HISTORIC HIKES IN WESTERN NORTH CAROLINA

NANCY EAST

Published by The History Press
An imprint of Arcadia Publishing
Charleston, SC
www.historypress.com

Front cover, top left: Albert "Dutch" Roth. *Courtesy of the Albert (Dutch) Roth Digital Photograph Collection, University of Tennessee Libraries; front cover, middle*: *Courtesy of Warren LeMay*; *front cover, top right*: Bertram Whittier Wells. *Courtesy of Hunter Library Special Collections, Western Carolina University; back cover*: *Courtesy of the Albert (Dutch) Roth Digital Photograph Collection, University of Tennessee Libraries.*

First published 2025

Manufactured in the United States

ISBN 9781467155663

Library of Congress Control Number: 2025931875

In memory of my beloved grandparents,
Paige and Dana Jones and Nancy and LeGrand "Lee" Mercure,
who instilled in me a love for adventure and a curiosity for the past.

CONTENTS

PREFACE

As a child growing up on the outskirts of Atlanta, Georgia, in the 1970s and '80s, I explored the woods behind my home regularly. A small creek bordered my parents' property, and beyond that was a wide clearing with electrical transmission towers that cut through the barren landscape as far as the eye could see. Amid the hum of electricity overhead, my neighborhood friends and I dared each other to explore the steel skeletons as far as they reached through the compacted red clay.

I don't remember ever making it to the end of the line, but I have vivid memories of a small abandoned home on the edge of the woods that usually halted our progress. Peering into the crumbling structure, I was particularly captivated by the peeling floral wallpaper that barely clung to the walls. Unlike my history classes in school, which largely amounted to memorizing facts and listening to my teachers' lecture, this small home brought history to life, even though I didn't know a single thing about its former occupants (over forty years later, I still wish I knew something about the family who lived in that home).

Nowadays, I often know in advance about historical artifacts I might encounter on a hike. While this removes some of the mystery, it makes for a more enriching experience. Knowing the history of a place or thing, whether natural or man-made, breathes new life into a hike, much in the way identifying a distant mountain peak or wildflower on the forest floor does. It also helps me appreciate what I might otherwise regard as a blemish on the landscape.

The first time I hiked the Tanawha Trail beneath the Blue Ridge Parkway's Linn Cove Viaduct, I was perplexed why a land management agency would choose to carve a footpath directly under the structure. After all, it was a massive man-made concrete structure, and I was there to experience the botanical and geological diversity of Grandfather Mountain.

When I began researching routes to include in this book, however, it was an easy decision to include that very hike. I learned the important role the viaduct played in the Blue Ridge Parkway's formation and how its engineers worked tirelessly to protect the flanks of Grandfather Mountain's ancient ecosystem while it was constructed.

On my next visit, instead of wanting to blast by the viaduct to get to the section of trail where man's imprint wasn't as noticeable, I marveled at this extraordinary feat of engineering, looking for the seams between sections while nodding my head in approval—the color of the concrete did, in fact, match the surrounding boulders.

Similarly, while I backpacked the Bartram Trail, the extent of my knowledge about William Bartram was that he was an eighteenth-century botanist who traveled throughout the southeastern United States on horseback and foot. I imagined this early explorer disrespecting Native culture and communities along the way, seeking to profit from his journey at the expense of others and the land. Bartram came to mean so much more to me when I learned of his amicable relationship with the Cherokee, built on a foundation of respect—something rare in those days between European explorers and Natives. Brent Martin writes in *The Changing Blue Ridge Mountains: Essay on Journeys Past and Present*, "I think of Bartram as America's first hippie and one of the only eighteenth-century Americans who still has groupies." Consider me a Bartram groupie now, too.

I have been hiking and backpacking in the mountains of western North Carolina for over three decades. This book comprises a collection of some of my favorite hikes that combine natural beauty with interesting historical relevance. Some of the hikes are popular, and you're likely to have company (pro tip: start early to avoid the crowds). But many of the routes aren't as well known and are relatively unmarred from the collective footprints of countless curious pedestrians.

It is my hope that some of the lesser-known routes maintain their sense of solitude or, at a minimum, are protected from the potential detrimental effects of visitors who don't adhere to "leave no trace" principles, whether from ignorance or otherwise. It is our individual choice to share these special spots we visit with others on social media or other websites, like blogs. If you choose to do so, please accompany your praise of the trail with a reminder to others of best practices while hiking. If you're not familiar with them, the Leave No Trace website is a great place to learn them (www.leavenotrace.org). I've also included a recommended list of hiking essentials to carry in your backpack and important steps to take before leaving home to facilitate a safe and enjoyable experience on the trail. Finally, don't skip over the chapter "How to Use This Book," as it details the best way to use the information in this book for an enjoyable (and safe) outing.

Also, hiking trails can change over time through natural or man-made alterations. The routes described in this guide were hiked shortly before Hurricane Helene caused significant damage to this region. As of this publication, repairs to roads and trails in Western North Carolina are ongoing. Before setting out, please verify that your planned route is accessible. Check the status of trails and roads with the relevant land management agency, via either their website or phone. Additionally, use a reliable mapping application, such as Google Maps, to confirm road access to trailheads. If you encounter discrepancies between your hike and the descriptions or waypoints provided in this guide, I would greatly appreciate your feedback. Your insights will help improve the accuracy of future editions of this guide.

Reach out if you'd like to share a story from your experiences on any of these hikes. One of the best parts of hiking is the community it fosters, and I'd love to hear from you!

Happy trails and safe returns,
Nancy East
www.nancyeast.com

ACKNOWLEDGEMENTS

Every book has an origin story. For this one, it came in the form of an email from my friend and mentor Danny Bernstein. Danny included me on a short list of authors whom she thought might be interested in writing a book for The History Press.

This book is only tangentially related to the initial idea The History Press presented, but I'd like to think it's one that will appeal to more history-loving hikers. Thank you, Danny, for believing in my abilities and recommending me.

Bob Plott, thank you for helping a complete novice learn how to interpret contracts, navigate archives and access useful photographs and documents related to this book. I am forever grateful for your kindness, friendship and knowledge.

Ken Wise, you were most helpful when I found some of my favorite photographs in the University of Tennessee Archives Albert "Dutch" Roth Special Collection. Thank you for connecting me with Charlie Roth. And Charlie Roth, thank you for allowing me to use your grandfather's beautiful work.

Many thanks to Pack Memorial Library, Transylvania County Library, Hunter Library at Western Carolina University and NC State University Library for your assistance in accessing photographs and your thoughtful encouragement.

I am grateful daily to the stewards of and the advocates for our public lands, particularly the Friends of the Mountains to Sea Trail, Benton

MacKaye Trail Association, Bartram Trail Conservancy, Appalachian Trail Conservancy, National Park Service, Conserving Carolina, Highlands-Cashiers Land Trust and Carolina Mountain Club. Thank you for all the good work you do to keep these trails alive and well and for your consent to use your photographs.

Speaking of photographs, a heap of thanks to the following people, who allowed me to showcase their talent: Misty Gilbert, Melissa Coatney, Steve Dickinson, Chris Marshburn, Adam Williamson, Esther Blakely, Steven Shattuck, Mel Gibson, Bev MacDowell, Andrew Renfro and Jordan Mitchell (hikewnc.info).

My father, Bill Mercure (aviator extraordinaire), was especially helpful deciphering aviation incident records with me, for which I am grateful. Thanks, Daddy.

My family may not always sense my gratitude, especially when writing deadlines supersede a homemade dinner, but they are who I am most grateful for every day. A special thanks to Larry, my husband, for being a constant soundboard and my number one fan.

Kate Jenkins, my acquisitions editor at The History Press, was exceptionally patient and kind, especially when I responded to her emails with "one more question"—that typically turned into five. Ashley Hill, my copy editor, was equally helpful during the final stages.

Writing is often a solitary endeavor, unless you count the company of your dog sleeping close by. Ivy was largely unfazed by the tapping of my keyboard and the occasional explicative spoken aloud when I realized three different sources differed in their account of a historical event I was researching.

Those were usually the times I stared out my office window to watch the songbirds (and a persistent chipmunk) at the bird feeder while taking a deep breath and contemplating why I was choosing to spend so much time and energy writing about these trails.

In some ways, the reason is selfish—I wanted to learn more for my own edification. However, equally true is that sharing my knowledge of Western North Carolina's trails with others brings me great joy. For that, I thank *you*, dear reader, for picking up this book. I hope that in doing so, it brings you joy, too.

THE TRAILS OF WESTERN NORTH CAROLINA

Trail Name	Distance	Difficulty	Views	Waterfalls	Kid-Friendly
1. Charlies Bunion	8.4 miles	Difficult	X		
2. Shuckstack Lookout Tower	7.0 miles	Difficult	X		
3. Noland Creek	9.1 miles	Moderate–Difficult	X		
4. Big Fork Ridge, Rough Fork Loop	9.5 miles	Difficult			
5. Cataloochee Divide	11 miles	Difficult	X		
6. Lakeshore Trail	5 miles	Easy			X
7. Little Cataloochee Trail	5.2 miles	Moderate			X
8. Oconaluftee River Trail	3.2 miles	Easy			X

Trail Name	Distance	Difficulty	Views	Waterfalls	Kid-Friendly
9. Cold Mountain	10 miles	Most Difficult	X		
10. Buck Springs Lodge	5.2 miles	Moderate	X		X
11. Catawba Falls	3.5 miles	Moderate		X	X
12. Cradle of Forestry	3.9 miles	Easy			X
13. Grandfather Profile Trail	7.4 miles	Most Difficult	X		
14. Hickey Fork/ Camp Creek Bald	10.8 miles	Most Difficult	X	X	
15. Laurel Creek	7.2 miles	Moderate			X
16. Mount Mitchell	5.5 miles	Moderate	X		X
17. Plott Balsams	5.4 miles	Moderate	X		
18. Rattlesnake Lodge	3.8 miles	Moderate	X		X
19. Linn Cove Viaduct	7.0 miles	Difficult	X		
20. Cheoah Bald	10 miles	Most Difficult	X	X	

Trail Name	Distance	Difficulty	Views	Waterfalls	Kid-Friendly
21. Joyce Kilmer Forest	1.9 miles	Easy			X
22. Whiteside Mountain	2.0 miles	Moderate	X		X
23. Yellow Mountain Lookout	12.2 miles	Most Difficult	X		
24. Cedar Rock/ Bridal Veil Falls	8.7 miles	Moderate	X	X	
25. Dupont Waterfall Loop	6.4 miles	Moderate		X	X
26. Bearwallow Mountain/ Wildcat Rock	7.9 miles	Difficult	X	X	
27. Bracken Preserve	8 miles	Difficult	X	X	
28. Carl Sandburg Home National Historic Site	varies	Easy–Moderate	X		X
29. Asheville Urban Trails	1.7 miles	Easy			X
30. Waynesville Public Art Trail	varies	Easy			X
31. Franklin Women's History Trail	varies	Easy			X

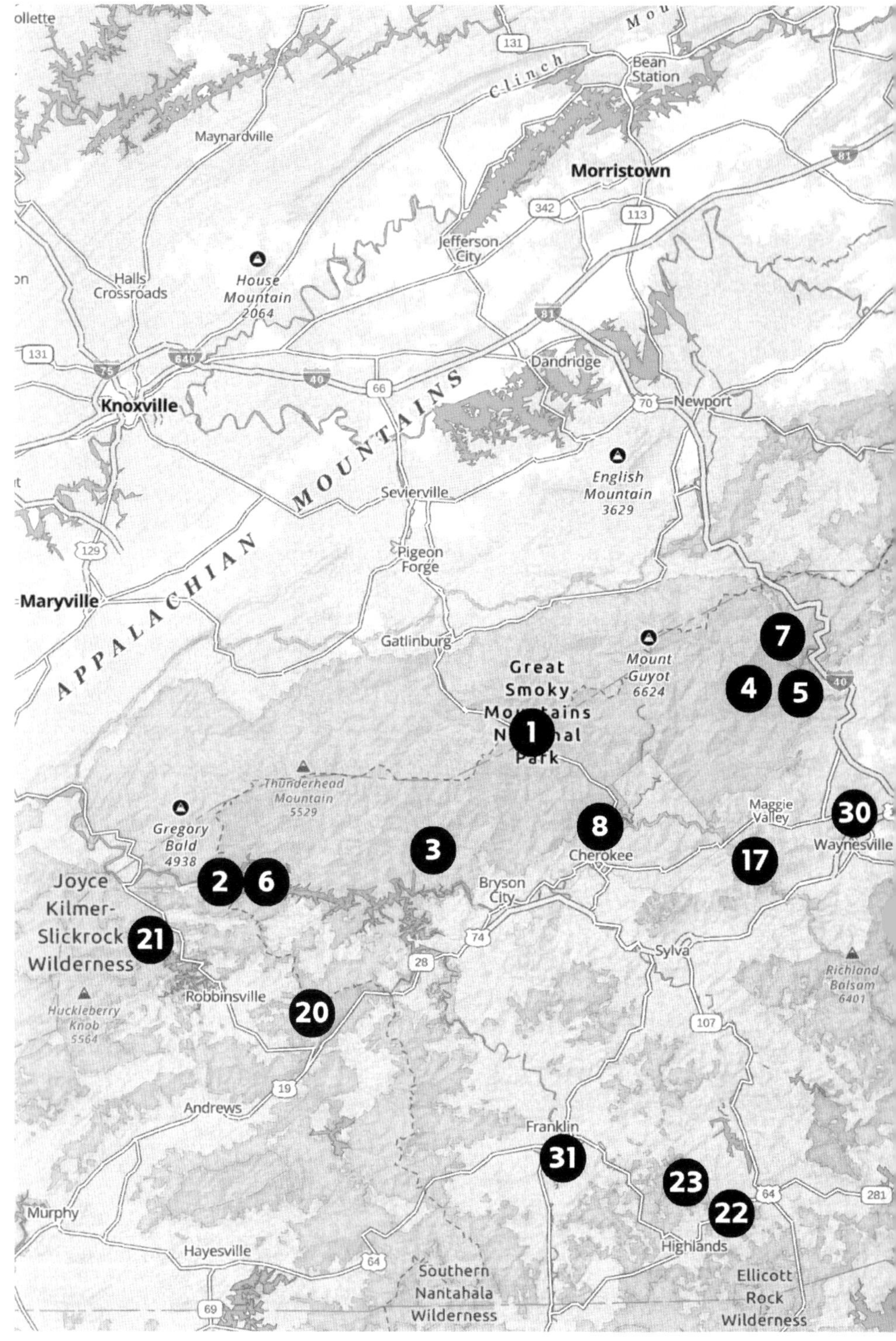

Maynardville
Clinch
Bean Station
Morristown
Jefferson City
Halls Crossroads
House Mountain 2064
Knoxville
Dandridge
Newport
APPALACHIAN MOUNTAINS
Sevierville
English Mountain 3629
Pigeon Forge
Maryville
Gatlinburg
Mount Guyot 6624
Great Smoky Mountains National Park
Thunderhead Mountain 5529
Gregory Bald 4938
Maggie Valley
Waynesville
Cherokee
Bryson City
Joyce Kilmer-Slickrock Wilderness
Sylva
Richland Balsam 6401
Robbinsville
Huckleberry Knob 5564
Andrews
Franklin
Murphy
Highlands
Hayesville
Southern Nantahala Wilderness
Ellicott Rock Wilderness

Big Laurel Branch Wilderness
Elizabethton
Johnson City
Elk Knob State Park
Jonesborough
Boone
Banner Elk
Blowing Rock
Erwin
Unaka Mountain 5180
Newland
Bakersville
Burnsville
Spruce Pine
Linville Gorge Wilderness
BLUE RIDGE
Mars Hill
Marshall
Morganton
Weaverville
Marion
Black Mountain
Old Fort
Asheville
Chimney Rock State Park
Fletcher
Spindale
Hendersonville
Forest City
Columbus
Brevard
Chesnee
Thicketty Mountain 1194
Inman
Pinnacle Mountain 3415
Travelers Rest
13
19
14
15
16
18
11
29
10
26
12
27
28
25
24

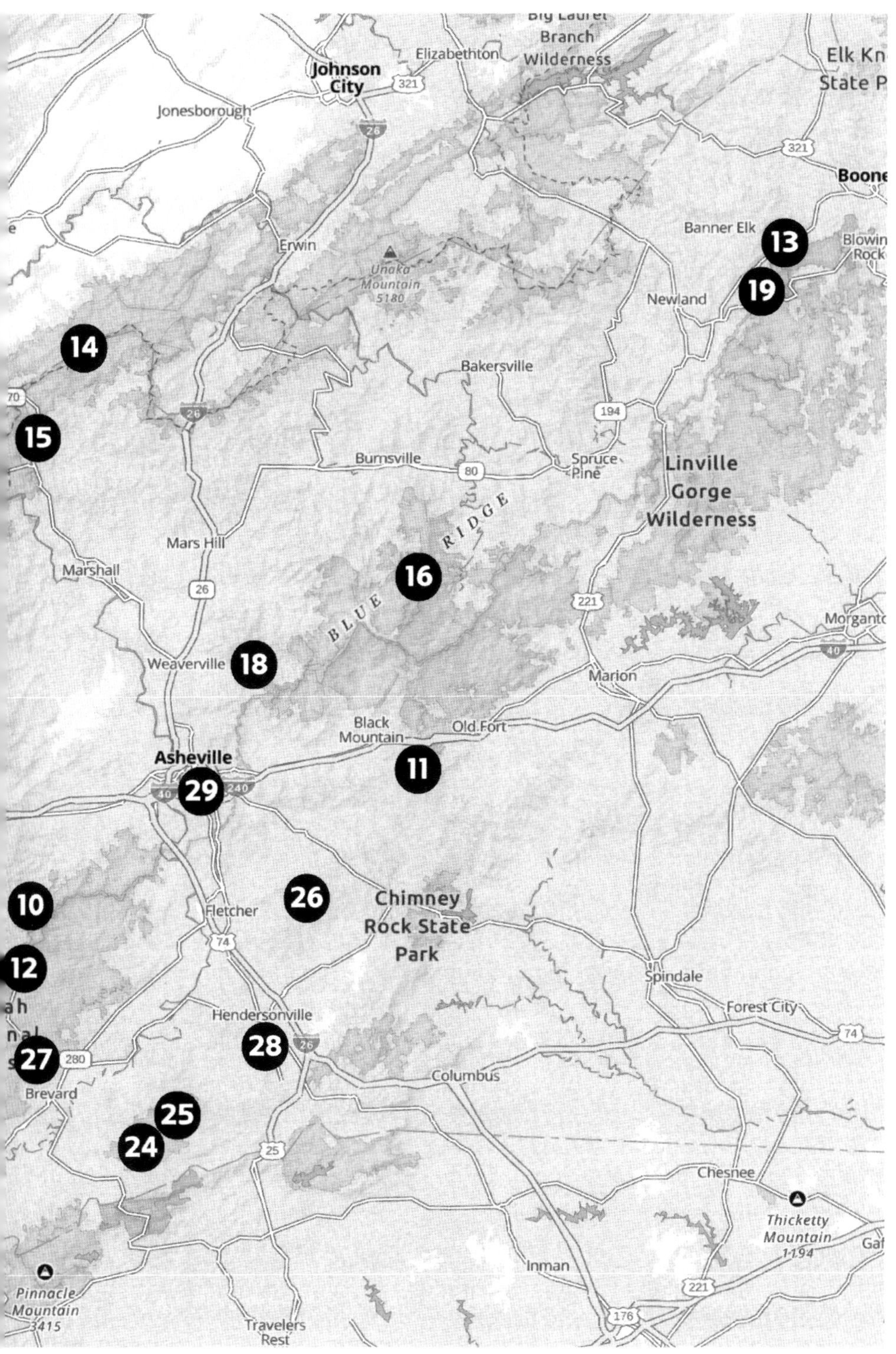

(HPBaseMap)

WHAT SEARCH AND RESCUE WANTS HIKERS TO KNOW

I have been a member of a search and rescue (SAR) team in Western North Carolina since 2015, and I've witnessed countless ways in which people end up needing help. A large percentage of these hikers could have avoided needing assistance (and enduring what is usually one of the scariest events of their life) if they had known how to plan better.

A short documentary film I helped produce, *Safe and Found*, can be found and viewed on the Jester Wallis Productions YouTube channel. It creatively explores the concepts of hiker safety and preparedness through stories of search and rescue.

WHAT TO BRING ON A HIKE

No matter how short your hike, I encourage you to *always* pack the "ten essentials." The ten essentials were originally assembled in the 1930s by The Mountaineers, a Seattle-based organization for outdoor adventurers, to prepare them for emergency situations outdoors. Now, the list has evolved to a "systems" approach. At first glance, it may seem excessive, but collectively, these items do not add up to much weight and can easily fit in a small backpack.

Every SAR operation I take part in is a lesson in discovery. Depending on our subject's situation, at least one of these items could have helped their predicament—if they had them in their possession. For those who didn't have them, my guess is that they don't leave home without them now.

1. Navigation: Map and compass, and knowledge of how to use them together. Apps such as Gaia GPS (my preference) are excellent tools for navigation, and I highly recommend having one downloaded on your phone to use on the trail; however, don't rely on them exclusively. Technology can fail, and it usually happens at the worst possible time.

2. Illumination: Headlamp and/or small flashlight. Extra batteries or a portable battery charger are also recommended.

3. First Aid: A first aid kit should be tailored to your needs. Mine includes over-the-counter pain medication and diphenhydramine (Benadryl), along with supplies to treat hot spots, blisters and minor wounds.

4. Gear Repair: This should also be customized to your potential needs. My repair kit includes a small supply of duct tape, dental floss, an embroidery needle, super glue and a small pocketknife.

5. Fire: Waterproof matches, a lighter and tinder.

6. Shelter: A heavy-duty trash bag that also doubles as a liner for your backpack can suffice. If the bag is used as an emergency shelter, a small slit can be cut in its side for ventilation.

7. Extra Food: Bring a little more food than you think you'll need in case you're out longer than anticipated.

8. Water: Bring an ample supply of water for the route you're hiking, but also have a plan for purifying more water.

9. Extra Clothing: Your clothing needs will vary depending on where and when you're hiking. Cotton clothing is not recommended for Western North Carolina—synthetics and wool are better choices. Make sure to always carry rain protection, even if rain isn't forecasted.

10. Sun Protection: Sunglasses, sunscreen and sun-protective clothing. A lightweight umbrella is also great for sun protection.

*Optional but highly recommended: A satellite device, such as a Garmin InReach Mini, or personal locator beacon, such as the ACR ResQLink. Some smartphones also have SOS and satellite messaging capabilities. If you are using your phone for photography and/or navigation, bring a portable battery charger. A loud whistle.

WHAT TO DO BEFORE LEAVING ON A HIKE

In addition to what you carry with you in your backpack on a hike, make sure to do the following before you leave home:

1. Leave an itinerary with someone and the estimated time you should be off the trail.

2. Check the weather forecast for the day of your hike and an additional two to three days beyond.

3. Research the area you'll be hiking in before you set out. Knowing your elevation gain and loss and learning about potential unbridged stream crossings and reliable water sources is valuable ahead of your hike.

4. Pack as if you'll spend a night waiting for a SAR team to come to your aid. If you're carrying the "ten essential systems," you should be in good shape.

5. Put your phone in airplane mode or turn it off while hiking in areas without cell reception (navigational apps work in airplane mode).

WHAT IF I GET LOST OR BECOME INJURED?

I'm so glad you asked! First, remember the acronym **STOP**. It stands for **S**top, **T**hink, **O**bserve and **P**lan. Stopping to think and act on logic rather than emotion after observing your environment and finding what you need to do to stay safe in it is a good way to plan during a stressful situation. Remaining stationary if you're truly lost, especially if you're on a trail, will allow SAR teams to come to your aid much quicker than if you are a moving target wandering through the woods.

One final item to pack doesn't cost or weigh a thing and will also help you if you become lost or injured: a positive mental attitude (PMA). I have consistently observed more favorable outcomes for our subjects who remain calm and optimistic about their predicament.

ENVIRONMENTAL HAZARDS AND WILDLIFE

Do your research so you can make informed decisions about mitigating risks from environmental hazards, such as weather-related events (thunderstorms, flooding, etc.) and possible wildlife encounters on the route you choose.

I have written extensively on my website (nancyeast.com) about these topics. Most trail conservancy websites also devote a section to these topics, as does the American Hiking Society's website.

HOW TO USE THIS BOOK

THE STATS

This section of each chapter is full of useful information to help you make an informed decision about a hike before setting out. You owe it to yourself (and those hiking with you) to understand how to use this information to your benefit and especially for your safety.

MILEAGE

The number stated is for the hike's overall mileage. Mileage is useful information, but it is only one piece of the puzzle when deciding on a suitable hike. Also, it is nearly impossible to accurately portray the exact mileage for a route between different hikers. If you track a hike, your mileage may vary slightly from mine, and that's not unusual. However, it should closely align with what the book indicates.

DIFFICULTY

There are myriad ways to gauge a hike's difficulty level, but there is also some degree of subjectivity in the assessment. Things I took into consideration while making my assessment were the distance of the hike, elevation gain and loss and the terrain type. I rated the hikes as easy, moderate, difficult and most difficult.

ELEVATION GAIN AND LOSS

Elevation gain and loss should be considered with a hike's distance, especially when estimating how long you'll need to complete a route. A good rule of thumb for most people is to count on hiking two miles per hour on flat terrain and adding an hour for each one thousand feet of elevation gained.

This "hiker math" does not include time for breaks, stopping to taking photographs, etc. Those factors are highly variable between individuals, but I encourage you to plan for more time than you think you'll need for them.

MAPS

In each chapter, in addition to the recommended paper maps that correspond to the hike, a topographic map image of the route is also included. Printable versions of these map images are available on my website at nancyeast.com/historyhikes.

You can either print these maps from my website on standard-size copy paper and/or upload the GPX file. My website also contains an elevation profile for each route. An elevation profile offers a sneak peek of what to expect with climbs and descents, and it is useful for assessing your abilities.

There are several excellent navigational apps that can help you stay oriented on trails, and I highly recommend downloading one of them and the associated maps for your hike before you leave home. My favorite is Gaia GPS. Digital apps and GPS devices, however, do not eliminate the need to *always* carry a paper map and a compass on a hike. Make sure you know the basics of reading a map and using a compass before your hike, too.

TRAILHEAD GPS COORDINATES

To use the set of coordinates provided, type the numbers (including the negative symbol in the second number) into a mapping app like Google Maps. Even if you follow the written driving directions provided, I recommend entering the trailhead GPS coordinates into a mapping app. This will alert you to any potential road closures, which is especially important as the region continues to recover from the damage caused by Hurricane Helene in September 2024.

HIGHLIGHTS

This section includes what I subjectively deem the best aspects of the hike.

NOTES

This section provides more logistical information in the hope of preventing any surprises when you reach a trailhead. This information includes potential fees, seasonal road closures, the presence of restrooms at a trailhead (or somewhere on the route) and whether dogs are allowed.

DRIVING DIRECTIONS

For luddites who eschew navigational apps while driving—or for the rest of us who recognize that technology will fail us at the most inopportune time—I've included turn-by-turn directions to each trailhead. Even if these directions are all you use while driving to the trailhead, I still encourage you to plug in the trailhead GPS coordinates I provide in each chapter to check for possible road closures.

WAYPOINTS

The numbered waypoints for each hike are meant to assist you with navigation. They are labeled on each chapter's corresponding topographic map image, and each number is added to the body of the hike description. Paying attention to these waypoints as you hike is another form of navigation referred to as dead reckoning. The printable maps available on my website (nancyeast.com/historyhikes) include these waypoints.

HIKE DESCRIPTION

Detailed turn-by-turn hiking directions are included in this section, as is any relevant history and information about the relics you may encounter along the way. For some of the routes, I included additional information following the hike description.

CONTINUING EDUCATION

This section includes my favorite books and films that complement the hike or area covered in each chapter. A full bibliography of sources used while I wrote this book can be found on my website (nancyeast.com).

TRAIL MAPS

Unless otherwise noted, the trail maps that appear at the start of each chapter are courtesy of @Gaia GPS @OpenStreetMap contributors and printable versions are available at nancyeast.com/historyhikes.

PART I

GREAT SMOKY MOUNTAINS NATIONAL PARK

1

APPALACHIAN TRAIL

CHARLIES BUNION

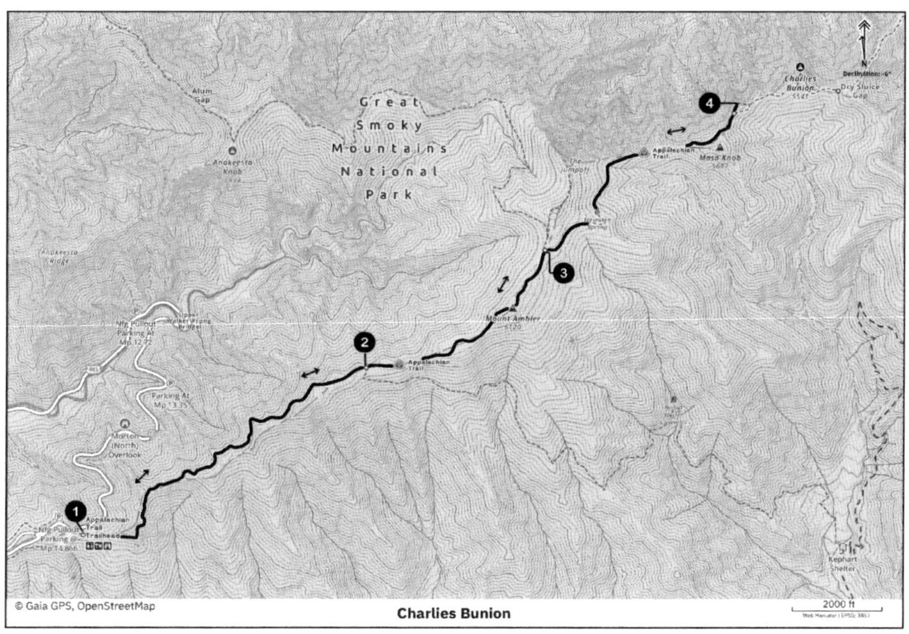

Charlies Bunion

OVERVIEW

Charlies Bunion (5,564 feet) is a wildly popular hike on the Appalachian Trail, and this is understandable given its spectacular high-elevation scenery. If you arrive early, you may have a bit of solitude—except for possibly crossing paths with an ambitious thru hiker heading either north to Maine's Mount Katahdin, nearly 2,000 miles away, or Georgia's Springer Mountain, "only" about 200 miles to the south.

You'll straddle the state line between North Carolina and Tennessee until you reach one of the most iconic rock outcrops in the Smokies—Charlies Bunion. From this unique perch, whose name has one of my favorite story origins in this book, you'll have a front-row seat to views of Mount LeConte and the Appalachian Trail's ridgeline as it heads north.

THE STATS

Distance: 8.4 miles out and back
Difficulty: Difficult
Elevation Gain and Loss: 1,900-foot gain, 1,813-foot loss
Maps: National Geographic no. 229 Great Smoky Mountains National Park; USGS 7.5' Mount LeConte Clingmans Dome, Mount Guyot
Trailhead GPS Coordinates: 35.61109, -83.42501
Highlights: Epic views, an iconic rock outcrop, spruce-fir forests, Appalachian Trail shelter
Notes: A parking permit is required to park a car for more than fifteen minutes anywhere in Great Smoky Mountains National Park. Permits can be purchased online or at kiosks and visitor centers around the park. There are seasonal restrooms at Newfound Gap and a privy at Icewater Spring shelter. Dogs are not allowed. There is a backcountry camping option at Icewater Spring shelter (by reservation). It's best hiked in late spring, summer and fall.
Driving Directions: From the Oconaluftee Visitor Center, drive north on Newfound Gap Road (US 441) 15.8 miles to the large Newfound Gap parking area on the right.

WAYPOINTS

1. Newfound Gap trailhead
2. Sweat Heifer Trail intersection (1.7 miles)
3. Boulevard Trail intersection (2.7 miles)
4. Charlies Bunion (4.2 miles)

HIKE DESCRIPTION

This hike begins on the Appalachian Trail (AT) at the base of the Rockefeller Memorial at Newfound Gap (**1**). Before you hit the trail, take a moment to explore the two-tiered curved stone monument and read its inscription. Calvin Coolidge signed a bill in 1926 that established Great Smoky Mountains National Park, but it wasn't until September 2, 1940, that Franklin Delano Roosevelt dedicated the new national park at this memorial.

During the fourteen-year interval, money had to be raised, and land had to be purchased from timber companies and private owners. In addition, park roads, trails and facilities had to be established. The monument was erected to recognize the generous $5 million donation from the Rockefeller family to help purchase land for the park.

> *In this park we shall conserve these trees, the pine, the red bud, the dogwood, the azalea, the rhododendron, the trout and the thrush for the happiness of the American people.*
>
> —*Franklin D. Roosevelt, park dedication at the Rockefeller Memorial*

President Franklin D. Roosevelt speaking at the dedication ceremony for Great Smoky Mountains National Park in 1940. *Tennessee State Library and Archives.*

At 0.6 miles, a view into North Carolina opens to the south. Continue your ascent amid the beauty of a spruce-fir forest, traveling over exposed rocks and roots.

At 1.7 miles, continue straight to stay on the AT and pass the Sweat Heifer Trail intersection on your right (**2**). At 2.7 miles, the Boulevard Trail departs to the left, heading to the summit of Mount LeConte (**3**). You'll pass below Mount Kephart's summit beyond the junction, and 0.2 miles later, a short spur trail on the right leads to Icewater Spring shelter. It's worth exploring the wood and stone structure, complete with a fireplace and bunks (there's also a privy nearby, should you need it). Beyond the shelter, you'll pass by its namesake spring before dropping in elevation on the trail. Then you'll reach a narrow ridge walk with steep drop-offs on either side.

At 3.6 miles, you'll begin skirting the left side of Masa Knob, named for George Masa, a Japanese immigrant and an early Smokies photographer. Often referred to as the "Ansel Adams of Southern Appalachia," Masa and his photography played an important role in inspiring the public to appreciate the need for this national park. He also played a critical role in the park's trail network, systematically measuring the trails and mapping the terrain.

Masa was a close friend of Horace Kepart, who was equally influential. Kephart's seminal work, *Camping and Woodcraft*, became an authoritative source for learning survival skills, campcraft and living harmoniously with nature. However, Kepart's tireless efforts in championing the preservation of wild spaces were his most lasting contributions. Masa and Kephart both relentlessly advocated for the creation of Great Smoky Mountains National Park.

Just over four miles into the hike, you'll reach an intersection. The AT continues to the right, but you'll follow the left spur trail, which will lead you across the North Carolina state line and barely into Tennessee. Continue down the spur to reach Charlies Bunion at 4.2 miles (**4**). You won't question if you've made it far enough when you arrive at a large rock outcrop that projects prominently from the left side of the trail, with an even larger and taller rocky knoll to the right.

Charlies Bunion earned its name when Charlie Conner, a local farmer and mountain guide, explored the area with Horace Kephart and George Masa in 1929. Masa and Kephart were on the North Carolina Nomenclature Committee, and they were charged with the task of naming various landmarks. The story varies slightly, depending on the source you read, but they all share a common thread of Conner complaining about his sore feet when he and Masa returned to camp after exploring the rocky

Left: Horace Kephart on top of Mount Kephart. *Buncombe County Special Collections, Pack Memorial Public Library, Asheville, North Carolina.*

Below: Hiker sitting on Charlies Bunion, admiring the distant views. *Photograph by the author.*

knoll. Kephart quipped, "Charlie, I'm going to get this place put on a government map for you!"

Charlies Bunion is a memorable place to take in the magnificent views to the north, prominent Mount Kephart and the Jump Off to the west, the more rounded curve of Masa Peak to the southwest and Mount Guyot in the east. Be especially mindful of your step; there are unforgiving drop-offs on all sides of the bunion if you venture out onto it.

When you're ready, continue following the spur trail as it curves to the right beyond the bunion. In about 0.1 miles, the spur trail bisects the AT. Turn right onto it and follow it back to Newfound Gap.

MARKING THE LEGACY OF MASA AND KEPHART

Study the map at the beginning of this chapter and look for a second marked location for Charlies Bunion northeast of the turnaround point for this hike. In the 1920s, the nomenclature committees were composed of local experts who were all vying for the chance to put their personal imprint on the names of the peaks in what would become Great Smoky Mountains National Park.

There were two committees, one for each state through which the AT weaves between the Smokies. Thankfully, both committees agreed on the clever name for the rock outcrop; however, the United States Geological Survey (USGS) mislabeled the location. They labeled it on their maps two ridges over, about a quarter mile from where Masa and Kephart indicated. You can still find this misprint on maps, many of which label the rock outcrop you are visiting as "the tourist bunion."

To further complicate matters, even the "tourist" bunion that people sit on and take their photographs from is likely not the same rock Masa and Conner explored. Ken Wise, a retired professor and Smokies historian at the University of Tennessee, Knoxville, proposes that the larger, taller knoll on the other side of the spur trail, directly across from the photogenic rock outcrop where visitors congregate, is what Masa and Conner likely designated as Charlies Bunion.

In 1939, James H. Caine of the *Asheville Citizen-Times* wrote: "When George Masa died some six years ago there was a movement afoot to fittingly recognize what he had done to preserve in pictorial history the scenic grandeur of the Great Smoky Mountains National Park. But like Mark Twain's weather, nothing has been done about it." Over three decades later, in 1960, the Carolina Mountain Club made progress with the USGS. In

George Masa on a mountainside with his camera. *Buncombe County Special Collections, Pack Memorial Public Library, Asheville, North Carolina.*

1961, one of the former "Fodderstack" peaks was named in Masa's honor, whose northwestern flank you will traverse on your hike to the bunion.

Neither Kephart nor Masa lived long enough to see their dream of a congressional charter for Great Smoky Mountains National Park come to fruition. Kephart died in 1931, when he was sixty-eight years old, in an automobile accident, and Masa died of complications from influenza in 1933, at the age of fifty-two. Masa was devastated after Kephart's death, and he requested to be buried beside his friend in Bryson City. Because he died penniless and funding for his grave was contingent on the kindness of his friends in the Carolina Mountain Club, Masa was buried in Asheville's Riverside Cemetery instead. But that the two men's namesake peaks are adjacent to each other in the land they cherished and fought for all of us to enjoy in perpetuity feels a more fitting tribute to their tremendous legacy.

CONTINUING EDUCATION

Ellison, George, and Janet McCue. *Back of Beyond: A Horace Kepart Biography*. Great Smoky Mountains Association, 2019.

Kephart, Horace. *Camping and Woodcraft*. Great Smoky Mountains Association, 2017.

Martin, Brent. *George Masa's Wild Vision: A Japanese Immigrant Imagines Western North Carolina*. Hub City Press, 2022.

The Mystery of George Masa. Documentary. Bonesteel Films, 2002.

2

APPALACHIAN TRAIL

SHUCKSTACK LOOKOUT TOWER

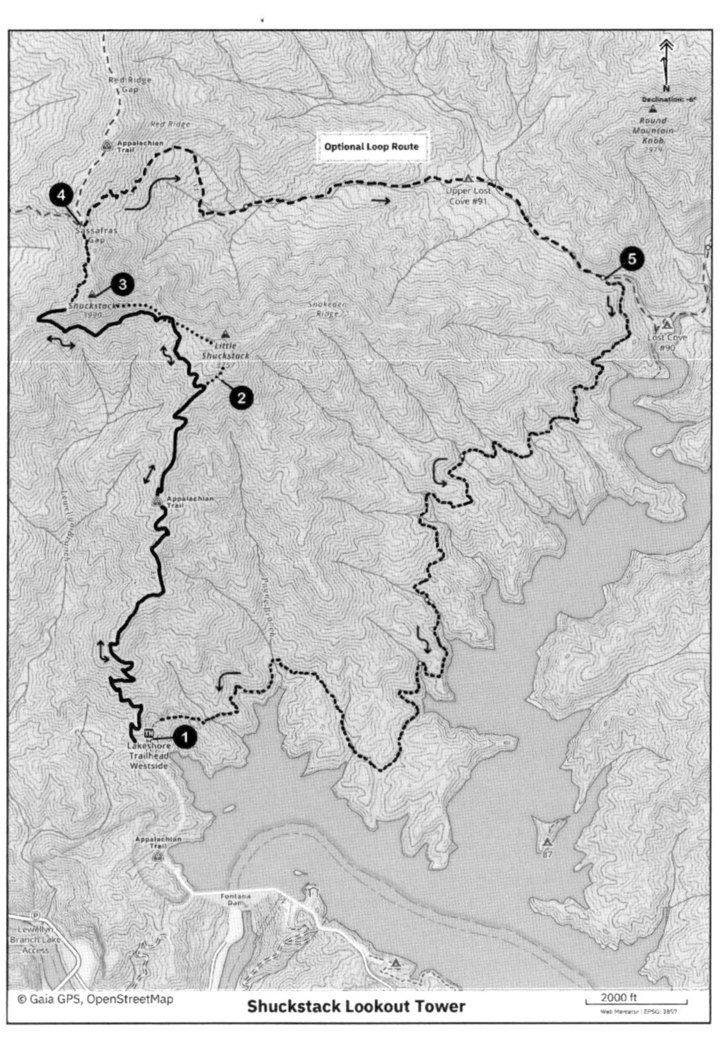

OVERVIEW

Shuckstack Mountain (4,020 feet), the peak on which its namesake lookout tower resides, got its name from its resemblance to a bundle of cornstalks when seen from a distance. On a clear day, as you are driving across Fontana Dam toward the trailhead, you can visualize the mountain and its tower high above you to form your own opinion about the shape. Regardless of your opinion, you will likely agree that this is a path worth traveling on the famed Appalachian Trail to visit one of the three remaining lookout towers in Great Smoky Mountains National Park.

THE STATS

Distance: 7.0 miles out and back (11.5-mile loop option)
Difficulty: Difficult (the loop option is Most Difficult)
Elevation Gain and Loss: 2,059-foot gain, 2,059-foot loss
Maps: National Geographic no. 229 Great Smoky Mountains National Park; USGS 7.5' Fontana Dam
Trailhead GPS Coordinates: 35.46043, -83.81107
Highlights: Hiking on the Appalachian Trail, epic and expansive views from the lookout tower's cab
Notes: This hike can be combined with the Lakeshore Trail hike in chapter 6 to create an 11.5-mile loop. The end of this chapter details the steps for the loop option. The loop option is not advised just after or during heavy rains, as Lost Cove Trail has several unbridged stream crossings that become hazardous with high water levels. A parking permit is required to park a car for more than fifteen minutes anywhere in Great Smoky Mountains National Park. Permits can be purchased online or at kiosks and visitor centers around the park. Dogs are not allowed.
Driving Directions: From Bryson City, travel west on NC 28 to Fontana Dam. Drive across the dam and then take a right at the fork, just past the dam. The parking area is about 0.6 miles from the dam.

WAYPOINTS

1. trailhead
2. junction of old Appalachian Trail route (2.1 miles)
3. spur trail to Shuckstack's summit (3.4 miles)
4. Lost Cove Trail intersection (3.9 miles)
5. Lakeshore Trail intersection (6.4 miles)

HIKE DESCRIPTION

From the trailhead (**1**), look for an information kiosk and the Appalachian Trail (AT) to the left of it. The white rectangular blazes that are painted on trees, all two by six inches, will mark your way, the first one visible shortly after you start. The trail gains elevation quickly and in earnest. Depending on the season and the leaf canopy, peekaboo views of Fontana Lake and possibly Shuckstack Tower will help take your mind off the climb. The trail maintains this upward trajectory until it makes a sharp left turn at 2.1 miles (**2**).

Before the 1970s, the AT continued straight with a punishing climb to the summit of Little Shuckstack Mountain. This summit also served as a fire lookout point for Montvale Lumber Company in 1917; however, there is no written record of a fire-watch structure on the peak. Montvale was a prominent timber harvesting company that had large landholdings in the region.

Now, instead of summiting Little Shuckstack, the AT veers left and the grade lessens, leading you to an exposed slate outcropping on Little Shuckstack's south slope. The trail along the outcropping is a wonderful place to stop, catch your breath and take a few photographs. The views to the south are wide open, and features such as Cheoah Lake; Canepatch Ridge, which extends down to the lake; and Sheep Knob to the west are all visible on a clear day.

After leaving the outcrop, the trail descends, but the reprieve doesn't last long. You'll soon begin another sharp ascent, this one leading you to the crest of Twentymile Ridge. At 3.4 miles, you'll arrive at the junction for the spur trail that leads to Shuckstack's lookout tower (**3**). Follow this winding uphill spur about 450 feet to the mountain's summit and tower.

Shuckstack's sixty-foot-tall steel tower was built by the Works Progress Administration in 1934, the same year Great Smoky Mountains National

Left: Albert "Dutch" Roth marking the Appalachian Trail, 1929. *Courtesy of the Albert "Dutch" Roth Digital Photograph Collection, University of Tennessee Libraries.*

Opposite, top: Shuckstack Lookout Tower under construction, 1934. *National Park Service.*

Opposite, bottom: Hikers taking in the view from the caretaker's cabin beside the Shuckstack Lookout Tower, 1936. *Courtesy of the Albert "Dutch" Roth Digital Photograph Collection, University of Tennessee Libraries.*

Park was officially established. A group of forty men from the Civilian Conservation Corps was assigned the task of building a three-mile truck road to Protector Field Gap and a two-and-a-half-mile trail to Shuckstack's summit. Later, between twelve and twenty-four men camped at Proctor Field Gap and walked to Shuckstack's summit each day to build the tower. Before the tower could even be built, a collective ten feet of rock had to be blasted from the mountain's summit to create a flat surface for it.

The rattlesnakes and copperheads the men discovered in the loose rocks afterward added an extra element of danger to the task. In November 1934, two and a half months after the construction of the tower and cabin began, the work was complete.

At the base of the tower are the remains of the tower keeper's one-room chestnut log cabin—a chimney, water cistern and foundation. The rest of the structure was removed in the 1980s. The one-thousand-gallon water

View of Fontana Lake from the Shuckstack Lookout Tower cab. *Photograph by the author.*

cistern collected rainwater from the cabin roof's gutters, and the water could be accessed internally using a hand pump. There was no indoor plumbing; a pit toilet was built downhill for that purpose.

If you don't have a fear of heights and exposure, climbing the tower's six flights of steps to reach its cab is an unforgettable experience. Your courage will be rewarded with an epic view.

From the cab, 360-degree views stretch out before you with minimal impact from human-built structures, aside from Fontana Dam and Lake. Fontana Lake is easy to spot to the south, with the Yellow Creek and Cheoah Mountains rising beyond it, including Cheoah Bald (4,062 feet), another prominent peak along the AT. To the east, High Rocks (5,190 feet) is visible, but the fire tower it once housed was removed in the 1980s, despite the tower keeper's deteriorating cabin remaining on site. The watchmen at High Rocks and Shuckstack Towers communicated via phone and radio to triangulate the location of smoke from fires. Gregory Bald, another iconic Smokies peak, can be seen to the west, while Thunderhead Mountain, Silers Bald and Kuwohi (formerly Clingmans Dome) all proudly line up before you in succession to the east.

Peter Barr, the author of *Exploring North Carolina's Lookout Towers*, was particularly inspired by Shuckstack Tower's views. In 2010, he thru hiked the AT and used the hike as a fundraising campaign for the tower's restoration, raising several thousand dollars for the cause. Nevertheless, it received only minimal repairs, and this iconic structure remains at risk of being removed by the park service due to safety and liability concerns.

> *The view from Shuckstack was as I remembered it: life changing. Nowhere else do I feel such a strong sense of belonging, such depth of meaning and attachment, than I feel at Shuckstack. This tower and this mountain altered the direction of my life. For this reason, I will never tire in my efforts to preserve it.*
>
> —*Peter Barr's Appalachian Trail journal,*
> *shared in* Exploring North Carolina's Lookout Towers

When you're ready to leave the tower, retrace your steps to the end of the spur trail. If you are hiking this route as an out-and-back endeavor, head back down the AT to the left, and you'll return to the trailhead where you started the hike in 3.6 miles. If you are hiking the 11.5-mile loop, see the following section for route details about this option.

APPALACHIAN TRAIL—LOST COVE—LAKESHORE TRAIL LOOP OPTION

This 11.5-mile loop is outlined with a dashed line on the map at the beginning of this chapter. From the junction of the Appalachian Trail and the spur trail that leads to the summit of Shuckstack Tower, veer right and head north on the AT. You are now walking on an old roadbed that was once used to access the fire tower by vehicles. The trail descends for 0.3 miles until it reaches Sassafras Gap and a four-way junction of trails (**4**).

Twentymile Trail feeds in from the left, but turn right and follow Lost Cove Trail, whose name's origin is unknown. The trail gets straight to work descending and is steep in places over the next mile. As you descend, look for enormous eastern hemlock trees in the forest. Because lumber companies did not have much use for these giants, they were usually spared from being felled.

These challenging steep slopes are replaced by multiple water crossings, starting with Lost Cove Creek. Some of these crossings become treacherous after heavy rains. As you hike between crossings, dog hobble and rhododendron take center stage, and partridge berry often blankets the forest floor. If you find partridge berry early in the season, look for a pair of diminutive white flowers scattered about its surface. Both flowers must be pollinated for edible red berries to grow. Two bright red spots will remain on the surface of the berries, a result of the fusion of the ovaries of the paired white flowers.

Also, be on the lookout for relics from the logging era of the early twentieth century. Montvale Lumber Company built a narrow gauge railroad up Eagle Creek with a spur on Lost Cove Creek. Remnants of a trestle can be found before the creek crossing above Upper Lost Cove Backcountry Campsite 91. It's also possible to spot cables left over from the logging days.

About 2 miles from the start of Lost Cove Trail, you'll arrive at Backcountry Campsite 91, which is the Will Messer homesite. In 1898, Messer purchased 283 acres in Lost Cove for $0.15 an acre, coming to a whopping total of $57.45. His original homesite was about 500 yards downstream, but this second site included a gristmill.

Few people inhabited this cove, however, given its terrain challenges. Look for the interesting birch tree stump in the middle of the campsite. Its stilt-like roots are the result of its seed initially germinating on the decaying "nurse log" of another tree. Eventually, the nurse log decomposed into the earth, leaving the leggy roots of the birch suspended in the air.

Beyond the campsite, you'll ford Lost Cove Creek several times before you arrive at the intersection with Lakeshore Trail, which you'll follow to the right and uphill (**5**).

Follow Lakeshore Trail for five miles back to the trailhead. Refer to the Lakeshore Trail hike in chapter 6 for more details about the history of this part of the route.

FONTANA DAM'S IMPACT ON THE APPALACHIAN TRAIL

Before Fontana Dam's construction (see chapter 6), the AT did not cover the ground you will walk on this hike. Instead, it descended from the Yellow Creek Mountains, crossed the Little Tennessee River on a highway bridge and entered the national park at Deals Gap on the park's western boundary. It went straight to work ascending Gregory Bald, which it now completely bypasses. The trail was rerouted in 1947 after the dam's completion.

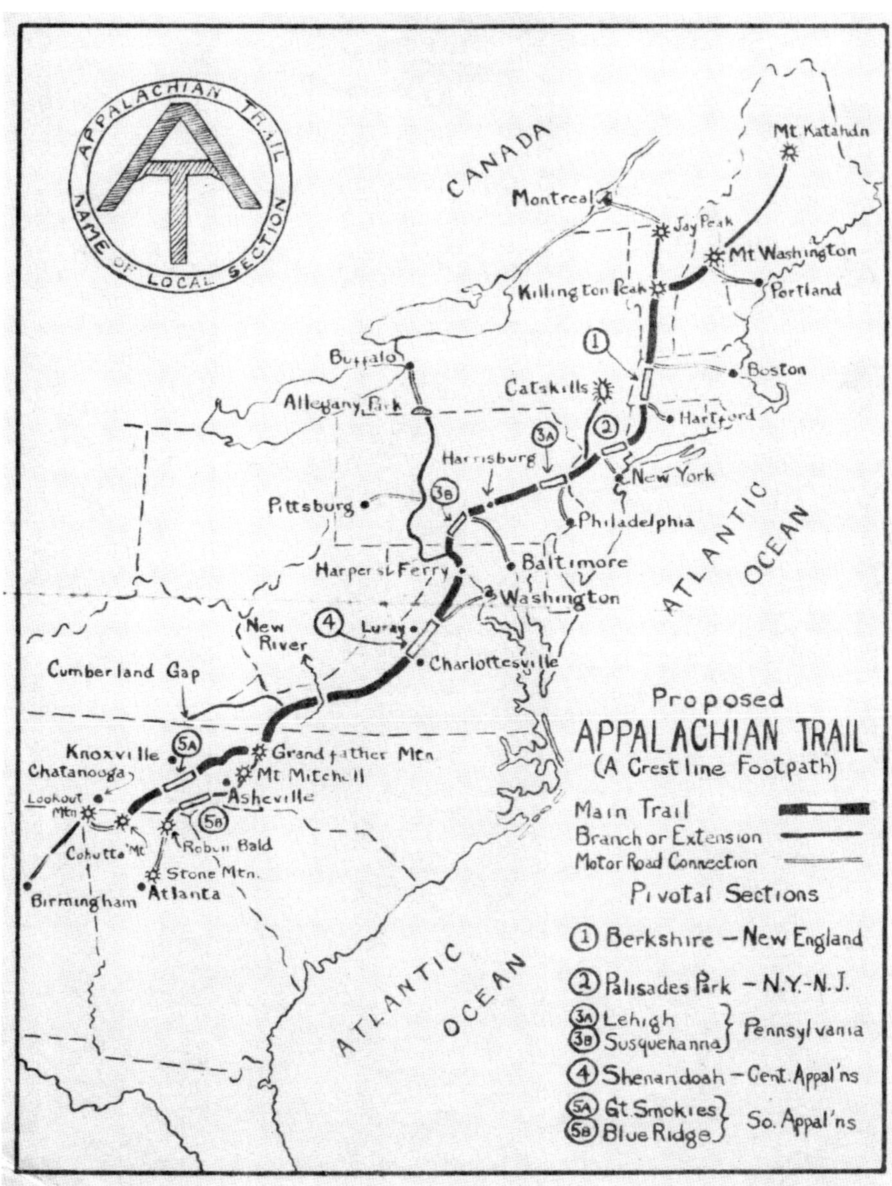

Map of the proposed Appalachian Trail, hand-drawn by Benton MacKaye for the first meeting of the Appalachian Trail Conference, March 1925. *MacKaye Family Papers, Rauner Special Collections Library, Dartmouth College.*

For Appalachian Trail thru hikers, this hike's trailhead symbolizes contrasting emotions depending on the person's direction of travel. For those perambulating north, it likely still represents the "honeymoon phase" of long-distance hiking, as they are only 164 miles into their nearly 2,200-mile journey; however, southbound hikers are only 164 miles from the trail's southern terminus on Georgia's Springer Mountain. These weary travelers are likely ready to "be there already"—the honeymoon phase having long since passed. Depending on the time of year, you may come across some of these dedicated adventurers on this hike. Wish them well and offer words of encouragement if you're lucky enough to meet one traveling in either direction.

CONTINUING EDUCATION

Barr, Peter, and Keith Adams. *Exploring North Carolina's Lookout Towers.* John F. Blair Publishers, 2021.

Harper, Ben. *Grandma Gatewood's Walk: The Inspiring Story of the Woman Who Saved the Appalachian Trail.* Chicago Review Press, 2014.

Wise, Kenneth. *Hiking Trails of the Great Smoky Mountains: Comprehensive Guide.* University of Tennessee Press, 2014.

3

BENTON MACKAYE TRAIL

NOLAND CREEK AND THE ROAD TO NOWHERE

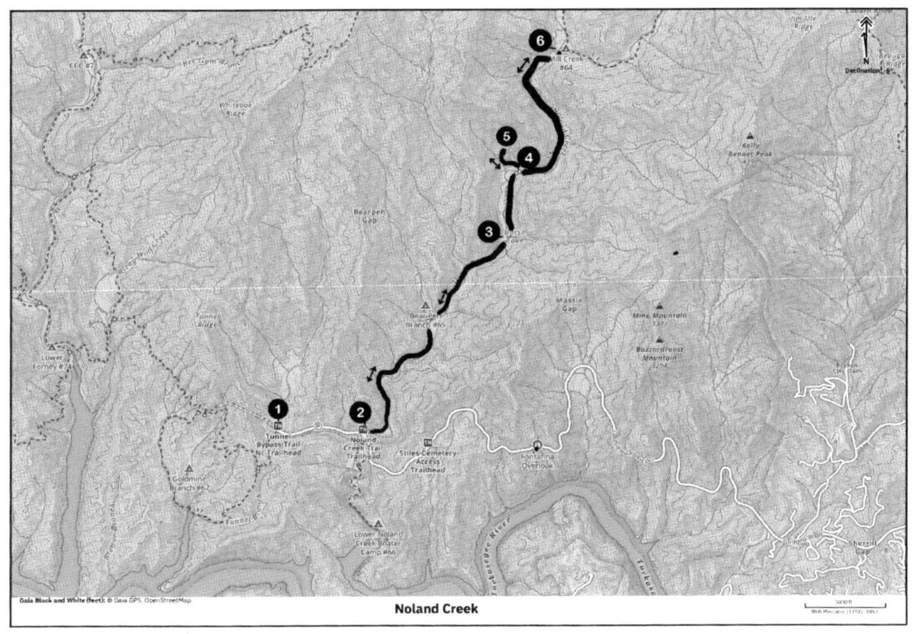

Noland Creek

OVERVIEW

Noland Creek Trail is part of the 288-mile-long Benton MacKaye Trail (BMT), which starts in the Big Creek area of Great Smoky Mountains National Park and ends on the summit of Georgia's Springer Mountain, which is also the southern terminus of the Appalachian Trail. The BMT spends nearly a third of its length in the national park, and this hike travels one of its easier segments, paralleling Noland Creek for a good portion it.

The area is rich with history, passing by several old homesites with easy-to-find relics, including the stone supports of waterwheels, chimneys and other foundational remains, along with one of my favorite cemeteries in the park, perched on a peaceful ridge. Because of its low elevation and wide, well-graded path, it's a wonderful hike nearly any time of year.

THE STATS

Distance: 9.1 miles (additional 0.4 miles for the recommended side trip and hike through the tunnel at the end of Lakeview Drive)
Difficulty: Moderate–Difficult (its distance may make it more difficult for some)
Elevation Gain and Loss: 932-foot gain, 932-foot loss
Maps: National Geographic no. 229 Great Smoky Mountains National Park; USGS 7.5' Noland Creek
Trailhead GPS Coordinates: 35.45820, -83.52690 (for Noland Creek Trailhead)
Highlights: The iconic and controversial Road to Nowhere and tunnel; a lovely, well-graded trail alongside melodic Noland Creek; unique historical structures; and an isolated ridgeline cemetery
Notes: A parking permit is required to park a car for more than fifteen minutes anywhere in Great Smoky Mountains National Park. Permits can be purchased online or at kiosks and visitor centers around the park. Dogs are not allowed.
Driving Directions: From Bryson City, take Lakeview Drive about eight miles to the Noland Creek Trail trailhead on the left. If you take the optional but recommended side trip to the tunnel at the end of Lakeview Drive, travel about another mile to the parking area just before the tunnel.

Waypoints

1. Lakeview Drive tunnel
2. Noland Creek trailhead
3. second wooden bridge and Arby Gass homesite (2.1 miles)
4. Ernest Lindsey homesite (2.6 miles); spur trail to cemetery (2.8 miles)
5. cemetery (3.1 miles)
6. fourth bridge and waterwheel remnants (4.0 miles)

HIKE DESCRIPTION

This adventure starts in your car along Lakeview Drive, commonly referred to as the "Road to Nowhere" (see *Road to Nowhere* at the end of this chapter). You'll dead end just before the famed tunnel that leads into the Smokies backcountry (**1**).

If walking through a dark, nearly quarter-mile-long tunnel doesn't spook you, it's worth the short out-and-back jaunt (bring a light source). The entrance makes for a fun and interesting photo backdrop, even if you don't venture inside. After leaving the tunnel, drive back the way you came in for a little more than a mile until you reach the parking area for the Noland Creek Trail on the right (**2**).

Your hike begins at the north end of the parking area, where you'll find a wooden engraved trailhead sign. Descend the steep hill beyond the sign, and you'll arrive at a T junction after a sharp switchback. To the left, Noland Creek Trail continues for a mile, with the creek spilling into Fontana Lake at the trail's end (and oftentimes before it if the dam-controlled lake is full).

Tunnel at the end of the "Road to Nowhere," 1996. *David Haas.*

Turn right onto the well-graded roadbed, which serves as the trail. In less than a quarter mile, pass under the Lakeshore viaduct and then cross a wooden bridge, the first of many you'll encounter on this hike. The trail you're walking on once led to a community of farmers, and this area was mostly spared from the detrimental logging industry. Cattle teams carried the logs to the mill at the end of Noland Creek rather than a logging railroad. There was also a portable mill much farther upstream.

It's debatable who Noland Creek was named for. Some claim it was named after William Noland, one of the first white settlers on the North Carolina side of the park in 1839. Late historian John Preston Arthur argued it was named after Andrew Noland, who lived at the confluence of Noland Creek and the Tuckasegee River. A local merchant from the village of Noland offered up the most entertaining of theories, however, when he postulated that the bottoms along Noland Creek are "no land, all rocks and no land."

Around 1.4 miles, the trail bears right. The path to the left leads to Bearpen Branch Backcountry Campsite 65, formerly the site of a schoolhouse. The Noland Creek community had two elementary schools, this schoolhouse and another that was located at Mill Creek. When the school at Mill Creek closed, Swain County commissioned a local resident to drive students from the upper Noland area down to the Bearpen school and back.

Just after you've hiked two miles, you'll cross a second wooden bridge. Shortly after, you'll encounter the first of several old homesites (**3**). A Bryson City baker, Arby Gass, once held property in this area. He planted several fruit trees, including apple, peach and pear trees. Lucky patrons benefitted from the bounty of his small orchard when he returned to his "city home" and stocked his bakery with fruit pies.

You'll encounter the site of Bob Patterson's home first. Boxwoods on the edge of the right side of the trail are your clue to look for the remains of a freestanding chimney on a small rise with a mature birch tree growing against it. Patterson was the Swain County sheriff, and he also ran a general store and post office up the trail.

At 2.6 miles, where the trail curves gently to the right, another clump of tall boxwoods heralds your arrival at a second homesite that was presumably owned last by schoolteacher Ernest Lindsey. There are extensive remains here, including large sections of the home's stone foundation. Even the stone steps that once led to the home's front door are remarkably intact, nearly hidden by the overgrown boxwoods flanking them. Opposite the stairs on the other side of the foundation, look for the concrete pad with pipes

Fieldstone chimney at the ranger patrol cabin site. *Photograph by the author.*

extending from its underside and a piece of round grating on top, along with scattered plumbing pipes.

Returning to the trail, and just past the third bridge, you'll walk past the former property of Phillip Rust, a wealthy landowner. After another 0.1 miles, take the side trail that feeds in from the left (**4**). Look for a path that angles sharply left and downhill toward a large fieldstone chimney after walking 0.1 miles on the side trail. Along with the nearly intact chimney are scattered relics, such as metal bed frames and plumbing pipes. An abandoned trap for catching invasive wild hogs also sits nearby. After the park inherited this property, rangers used it to patrol the Noland Creek drainage until 1979, when it burned down. Some believe the fire was started by hunters who weren't keen on rangers keeping watch over them.

Head back up the hill from the chimney and turn left to continue following the spur trail that leads steeply uphill for another 0.2 miles. The path swings widely to the right and ascends to a narrow high ridge where about a dozen graves rest (**5**). Unmarked headstones are coupled with more modern engraved markers; however, the dates of birth and death are missing from them. Especially poignant is the last grave; its inscription reads, "Known but to God." It's a peaceful spot for reflection.

Retrace your steps back to Noland Creek Trail and turn left. You are now walking through Salola Valley as you head toward the fourth bridge. It's believed that the valley got its name from the Cherokee word salali, which means "squirrel."

Four miles in, you'll cross a fourth bridge. Just before the bridge, there is a faint path to the left that leads to a concrete base and ten-foot-tall stone supports for a waterwheel (**6**). Rust, the property owner who lived a mile back, used the waterwheel to generate electricity, a rarity during this era, for an electric fence that surrounded a six-hundred-acre sheep pasture. It's believed the waterwheel also served as a gristmill for the community.

In another 0.2 miles, you'll cross a fifth bridge just before you arrive at the junction of Springhouse Branch Trail and Backcountry Campsite 64. The large campsite, frequently used by horseback riders, has picnic tables and is a fine place to stop for a snack. Notice the bear cables in the campsite, which backpackers use to hang their food to protect it from wildlife. This is the turnaround point for the hike. Retrace your route on Noland Creek Trail for 4.2 miles back to the trailhead and enjoy the mostly downhill journey.

ROAD TO NOWHERE

Lakeview Drive, which offers great aerial views of Fontana Lake and the Tuckaseegee River, harbors the contentious nickname of "Road to Nowhere." In the 1960s, construction began on this road in response to a promise the government made following the creation of Fontana Dam (see chapter 6, "Lakeshore Trail and Fontana Dam").

If the road's construction had been carried out as promised, it would have continued past the tunnel and paralleled Fontana Lake's north shore all the way to Fontana Dam. Environmental concerns, such as severe erosion and acidic runoff impacting fisheries in many streams, halted the project. The tunnel is where the road ended, hence its moniker. In late 2000, Congressman Charles Taylor and Senator Jesse Helms obtained $16 million in federal funding for the completion of the road; however, even with this funding, the project did not come to fruition, partly because of the proposed construction costs.

For many families, the incomplete road presented an enormous challenge to visit the cemeteries and old homesteads where their ancestors once lived. In 1978, the North Shore Cemeteries Association was formed, organizing decoration days for over twenty cemeteries situated on Fontana Lake's north shore. Initially, the association had to use its own resources to cross the lake by boat and then walk to the cemeteries. Eventually, the park service became more involved in assisting with the effort, providing boat services and ATVs along with trail crews to help the families reach the more remote cemeteries.

In 2007, Swain County was promised $52 million as a settlement for the incomplete road, which approximated the costs of finishing the road in 1943, plus interest. The full amount of this settlement was not granted until 2018, however. The settlement money is now held by the state, but Swain County benefits from the interest annually.

Even though the road was an understandable loss to many, it created a portal to explore one of the most remote stretches of the national park's backcountry. Lakeshore Trail starts beyond the tunnel and meanders above Fontana Lake before it emerges thirty-five miles later near Fontana Dam.

BENTON MACKAYE AND HIS NAMESAKE TRAIL

Benton MacKaye (1879–1975) was an American forester, planner and conservationist best known as the visionary behind the Appalachian Trail. Born in Stamford, Connecticut, MacKaye earned the first forestry degree at

Harvard University and established himself as a pioneering figure in the field.

In 1921, following the tragic suicide death of his wife, Jessie "Betty" Hardy Stubbs, a notable suffragist, MacKaye wrote a seminal sixty-page article, titled "An Appalachian Trail: A Project in Regional Planning." In the memorandum, MacKaye proposed a continuous hiking trail along the Appalachian Mountains, connecting Mount Washington in New Hampshire to Mount Mitchell in North Carolina. The trail, completed in 1937, would serve as a corridor for recreational, cultural and economic activities, providing a place for people to escape urban life and experience the wilderness.

> *Life for two weeks on the mountain top would show up many things about life during the other fifty weeks down below.... There would be a chance to catch a breath, to study the dynamic forces of nature and the possibilities of shifting to them the burdens now carried on the backs of men.*
>
> —*Benton MacKaye, 1921*

MacKaye's visionary ideas didn't end after the Appalachian Trail became a reality. He wrote extensively on topics related to forestry, conservation and urban planning, and he remained dedicated to environmental and social causes. He had a reputation for being uncompromising with his viewpoints, sometimes to the point of resigning from his various positions out of frustration.

In 1975, the seeds of the Benton MacKaye Trail were sown when Dave Sherman, a founding member of the Benton MacKaye Trail Association (BMTA) became intrigued by MacKaye's proposals for additional spur trails to branch southward from the AT. Sherman envisioned a new trail tracing the high ridge along the Tennessee–North Carolina border, bridging the Smoky Mountains and the Cohutta Mountains in northwest Georgia. The route would then proceed eastward, ultimately reaching its terminus at Springer Mountain.

The notion of creating a sister trail to the AT, eventually named after Benton MacKaye, gained traction and led to the formal establishment of the Benton MacKaye Trail Association in 1980. Functioning as an all-volunteer force, the BMTA collaborated closely with the U.S. Forest Service to commence trail construction. Initial efforts focused on Georgia, gradually

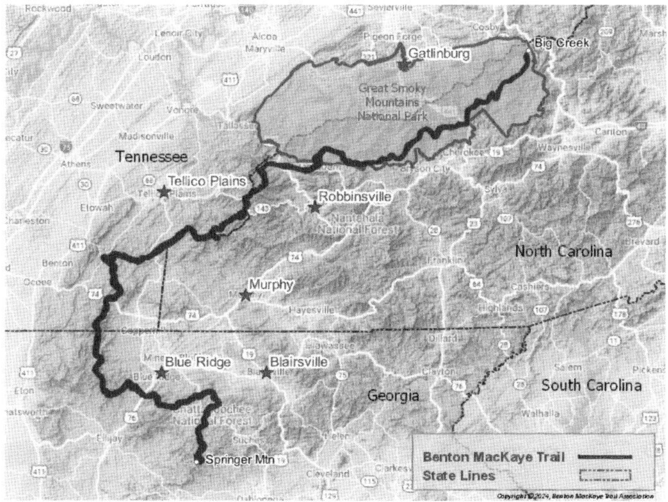

Opposite: Benton MacKaye, 1931. *Appalachian Trail Conservancy.*

Left: Map of the Benton MacKaye Trail. *Benton MacKaye Trail Association.*

extending along the Tennessee–North Carolina border and, ultimately, reaching the Smokies.

The BMTA leveraged existing trails and repurposed old logging roads to create the footpath. By 1989, the trail had reached Double Spring Gap on the Georgia-Tennessee line. For the next fifteen years, the association embarked on a substantial initiative to connect the trail to the Smokies. Following this achievement, the National Park Service collaborated to chart a route through the park.

The culmination of these dedicated efforts occurred in 2005, thirty years after Dave Sherman's initial vision, marking the completion of the 285-mile-long Benton MacKaye Trail. While it's not nearly as popular as the AT and has far less foot traffic, it is likely reminiscent of how the AT once felt. Nowadays, an average of three thousand hopeful backpackers attempt to walk every step of the AT's nearly 2,200 miles annually, with only about a quarter of them successfully completing the lofty goal. Additionally, over three million visitors amble along it for a shorter distances and durations.

CONTINUING EDUCATION

Anderson, Larry. *Benton MacKaye: Conservationist, Planner, and Creator of the Appalachian Trail.* Johns Hopkins University Press, 2002.

Strutin, Michael. *History Hikes of the Smokies.* Great Smoky Mountains Association, 2012.

4

BIG FORK RIDGE, ROUGH FORK LOOP

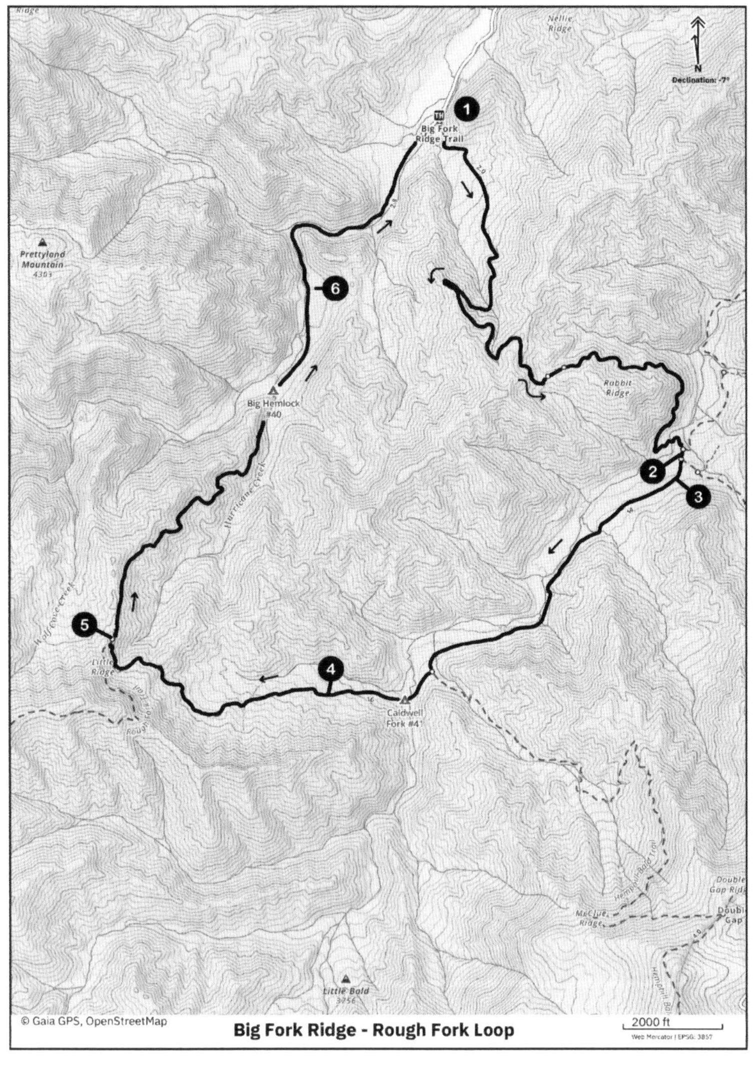

Big Fork Ridge - Rough Fork Loop

OVERVIEW

My favorite season to take this hike is in the fall, during the elk mating season, also known as the rut. The bulls boisterously vie for the attention of the cows and aggressively guard their harem from the attentions and advances of other bulls. It's quite a show, but you'll miss it if you're not in the valley at dawn or dusk, since elk are crepuscular, which means they're most active during these times. They retreat to the cooler canopy of the nearby woods as the day warms up.

This hike is a good option if you have children who can handle the nearly ten-mile trek. Make sure to reserve some time to also explore the historical structures in Cataloochee Valley, such as Palmer Chapel, Beech Grove School and the Caldwell House.

THE STATS

Distance: 9.5-mile loop
Difficulty: Difficult
Elevation Gain and Loss: 1,813-foot gain, 1,741-foot loss
Maps: National Geographic no. 229 Great Smoky Mountains National Park; USGS 7.5' Dellwood, Bunches Bald
Trailhead GPS Coordinates: 35.61694, -83.11990
Highlights: Smokies history and historical structures; possible wildlife sightings, such as elk; old-growth forest
Notes: A parking permit is required to park a car for more than fifteen minutes anywhere in Great Smoky Mountains National Park. Permits can be purchased online or at kiosks and visitor centers around the park. Check for road closures in the Cataloochee Valley area during winter. Dogs are not allowed on the backcountry trails, but leashed dogs are allowed in the valley. Flushable toilets are available at Cataloochee Campground, and pit toilets are located at the Pretty Hollow Gap trailhead.
Driving Directions: From Interstate 40, take exit 20 (U.S. 276) and turn right onto Cove Creek Road. Follow it for ten miles over Cove Creek Gap and into Great Smoky Mountains National Park. At the four-way intersection, turn left and follow this road six miles to the end of the road.

WAYPOINTS

1. trailhead
2. Caldwell Fork Trail junction (3.2 miles)
3. Shelton and Caldwell graves (3.3 miles)
4. big poplar tree (5.0 miles)
5. junction with Rough Fork Trail (6.3 miles)
6. Woody home (8.3 miles)

HIKE DESCRIPTION

This hike starts at the end of the road that takes you through Cataloochee Valley. Along the drive to the trailhead, you'll pass through bucolic meadows where the elk descend around sunrise and sunset. Otherwise, they usually take shelter in the forests, so be aware of this as you hike. As with any wildlife, stay a minimum of twenty-five yards away. To gauge this distance, use the "rule of thumb" method, which entails holding your thumb up in front of the wildlife. If your thumb obscures your view of the animal, you're probably a suitable distance away from them.

From the parking area (**1**), walk down the road you drove in on for less than a tenth of a mile and look for the Big Fork Ridge trailhead sign on the right. The trail immediately crosses a log footbridge over Rough Fork, entering the former homesites of members of the Caldwell family. Though the structures are gone now, you'll also pass by the former location of the holding pens for the elk when they were reintroduced to the park in 2001.

The trail now begins climbing in earnest, often on a rocky, rutted path. Red maple, white pine and eastern hemlock rise above you initially, but they are eventually replaced by mountain laurel and rosebay rhododendron. If you're hiking in fall, look for striped maple trees. They're easy to spot because their yellow-green three-lobed leaves take on a more transparent appearance, loosely resembling a ghost or a goose foot (one of their nicknames is goosefoot maple).

At the one-mile mark, the trail bears right and levels off when it reaches a narrow ridge. To the left of the ridge are a multitude of dying or dead eastern hemlock trees, victims of the hemlock woolly adelgid. Over eight hundred acres of old-growth hemlock trees grow in the national park, but their numbers have been greatly impacted by the adelgid.

The aphid-like insect made its way into North America in the 1920s, and they are easily recognizable at the base of hemlock needles because they look like tiny cotton balls. The white, waxy "wool" that gives these insects their distinctive appearance is their protective coating. They feed on the sap of a tree through the base of its needles, which disrupts the tree's nutrient flow. The needles eventually fall off, causing the tree to starve within three to five years. The aphid prefers to attack mature hemlocks.

Different types of treatments are being implemented by the National Park Service to control the adelgid's destruction. Insecticidal soaps are sprayed onto trees, but this method requires repeated treatment every six months to a year. The more popular method involves insecticides like those used in flea and tick medication for dogs. The insecticide is injected into the tree or mixed with water and poured around the trunk. Nearly two hundred thousand trees have been treated this way in the park. Predator beetles are a third method of control. By 2011, the park had released over half a million beetles for this purpose. The measurable effect of this approach takes more time to quantify, but the preliminary results are encouraging.

At the 1.8-mile mark, you will crest the top of Big Fork Ridge. From here, you'll start to descend as you make your way around Rabbit Ridge. At 3.1 miles, cross Caldwell Fork on a long footbridge, and a few hundred yards later, you'll reach the junction with Caldwell Fork Trail (**2**).

At this three-way intersection, bear right onto Caldwell Fork Trail. In less than a tenth of a mile, stay right at the junction with McKee Branch Trail to remain on Caldwell Fork Trail. This area was once the site of the Caldwell Community School. Children were expected to help with farmwork, so they usually attended school for only five months each year from 8:30 a.m. to 3:30 p.m. On Friday evenings, Caldwell Fork residents would gather at the school with the children to hear them recite poems and give speeches.

In another tenth of a mile, look for a "No Horses" sign on the left side of the trail with a steep side trail near it. Climb this short trail for about one hundred feet, and you'll reach a small gravesite with two stone markers (**3**).

Brothers-in-law Levi Shelton and Ellsworth "Elzie" Caldwell were murdered near this site on April 1, 1865, by Colonel George Kirk, a Confederate deserter and infamous Union raider known for his regiment's guerrilla-like tactics. Kirk, along with four hundred cavalry and two hundred foot soldiers, descended on Cataloochee Valley and wreaked havoc. The remote valley had established its reputation as a hiding spot for AWOL soldiers. Many of the valley residents didn't hold allegiance to either side of the Civil War and resisted fighting in a war that did not serve them. They were fiercely independent, and the only fight they were interested in was the one to sustain the hardscrabble lives they'd carved out for themselves.

Kirk and his raiders whipped Shelton and Caldwell's wives in an attempt to force them to disclose the men's hiding place. These strong women held their secret, despite the beatings. Kirk and his men waited until after dark and followed the women to their husbands' hiding place. Shelton and Caldwell were captured and executed, and their bodies were covered with chestnut bark after they were thrown in a sinkhole between Rough Fork and Caldwell Fork. The bodies were later retrieved and buried in the same grave where you will now be standing. The inhabitant of the second grave marker is allegedly a woman whose identity is unknown.

Backtrack to Caldwell Fork Trail from the gravesites and turn left onto it. At four and a half miles, cross Double Gap Branch, and in another tenth of a mile, Hemphill Bald Trail will take off to the left. After you cross Caldwell Fork on a log footbridge, you'll pass the Caldwell Fork Backcountry Campsite 41, which boasts a tranquil creekside setting and is one of my favorite backcountry campsites in the park. The Sutton family kept milk cows here. They cleared three steep hillsides near the site for farming and claimed you could "dig out 'taters and just let 'em roll down the hill."

Continuing to the five-mile mark, you'll see a sign that reads, "Big Poplars." Take this short detour to the right, and soon, you'll be standing in front of the most prominent "big poplars" the sign refers to (**4**). *Liriodendron tulipifera*, which are actually in the magnolia tree family and not poplars at all, were commonly felled to build structures, such as houses and barns, thanks to their trunks' straight anatomy. The tree indicated on the sign is at least twenty-five feet in diameter. If you're with a group, see how many people it takes to encircle the tree while still touching fingertips. There are a few more large poplars behind this one, but this is the biggest.

Return to the main trail and take a right to head uphill on a mostly gentle grade. At 6.3 miles, you'll reach the intersection with Rough Fork Trail, where you'll turn right again (**5**). Your efforts in climbing will now be rewarded with a long descent. Eventually, you'll hear Hurricane Creek rushing to your right, and around the 7.8-mile mark, you'll pass the side trail that leads into the Big Hemlock Backcountry Campsite 40 and rock hop Hurricane Creek shortly after. Around mile 8.3, the Woody home and springhouse come into view (**6**).

The Woody residence had more humble beginnings than the charming two-story home you'll visit on this hike. It was initially a one-room log cabin built in 1851 by Jonathan Woody. Over the years, its size expanded—and for

Left: Levi Shelton and Ellsworth Caldwell's grave. *Photograph by the author.*

Below: Backpackers exploring the Woody home and grounds. *Photograph by the author.*

Stump of a large tulip tree, 1926. *National Park Service.*

good reason. At one point, fourteen children lived in the home. One of those children, Steve Woody, who was known to ride only a black horse, lived in it until two years before his death in 1942. The Woodys were farmers, and the land that surrounded the home was cleared extensively. The interior of the home is now open to explore, so be sure to step inside. There are three bedrooms downstairs and three more upstairs, as well as a kitchen and two fireplaces. Note the differing heights of the ceilings—evidence of additions to the home over time. A large juniper tree in the front yard takes center stage.

After leaving the Woody property, continue following Rough Fork Trail, which becomes an old roadbed and crosses three log footbridges. You'll reach the end of the trail after walking another mile on one of the flattest stretches of trail in the entire park.

ELK REINTRODUCTION IN GREAT SMOKY MOUNTAINS NATIONAL PARK

Most people don't think of the southern states when they think of elk; however, elk once roamed much of the continental United States. It's believed that by the late 1700s, the last elk in North Carolina had been killed. By 1900, North American elk were at risk of becoming extirpated due to overhunting and a loss of habitat.

The National Park Service's mission is to preserve native plants and animals on the land it manages. On occasion, attempts are made to reintroduce a native extirpated species. But sometimes, the reintroduction of a species doesn't go as well as the park service hopes, and those projects are suspended. The reintroduction of the red wolves in Great Smoky Mountains National Park is one such example.

Despite this unsuccessful attempt, the park has successfully reintroduced other species, such as the peregrine falcon and river otter. In 2021, a reintroduction of elk was instituted when twenty-five elk were bought from the Land Between the Lakes National Recreation Area along the Tennessee-Kentucky border. A year later, another twenty-seven elk were brought in from Elk Island in Manitoba, Canada.

The reintroduction had its struggles, however, such as black bears preying on the calves, which threatened the success of the program. Eventually, the bears were temporarily relocated to a different part of the park, over forty miles away, until the calves were old enough to escape the apex predator. A North Carolina–based delicacy, Krispy Kreme doughnuts, were part of the bait to lure bears into the traps.

Bull elk in Cataloochee Valley. *Esther Blakely.*

This practice sparked controversy, as some believed park biologists shouldn't intervene with natural selection, while others feared the valley would be devoid of bears in the future. It proved to be a beneficial move for both the elk and bears. Within two weeks—enough time for the growing calves to better fend for themselves—many of the tagged bears had ambled back into the valley, their internal GPS systems having led the way.

Ultimately, the program was successful, and around two hundred elk are now thriving in North Carolina, mostly in the western portion of the state. Wildlife biologists believe about half of the population lives within the national park's boundaries.

ALTERNATE ROUTE

If you'd rather spend more time in Cataloochee Valley, visiting the historic structures, than hiking the loop route described in this chapter, a shorter out-and-back hike on Rough Fork Trail to the Woody home is a worthwhile journey. This is also a more suitable route for younger children, since it's only two miles round trip.

CONTINUING EDUCATION

Caldwell, Wayne. *Cataloochee.* Random House, 2007.

Houk, Rose. *Rocky Mountain Elk: Return of the Native.* Great Smoky Mountains Association, 2005.

5
CATALOOCHEE DIVIDE TRAIL TO THE APPALACHIAN HIGHLANDS SCIENCE LEARNING CENTER

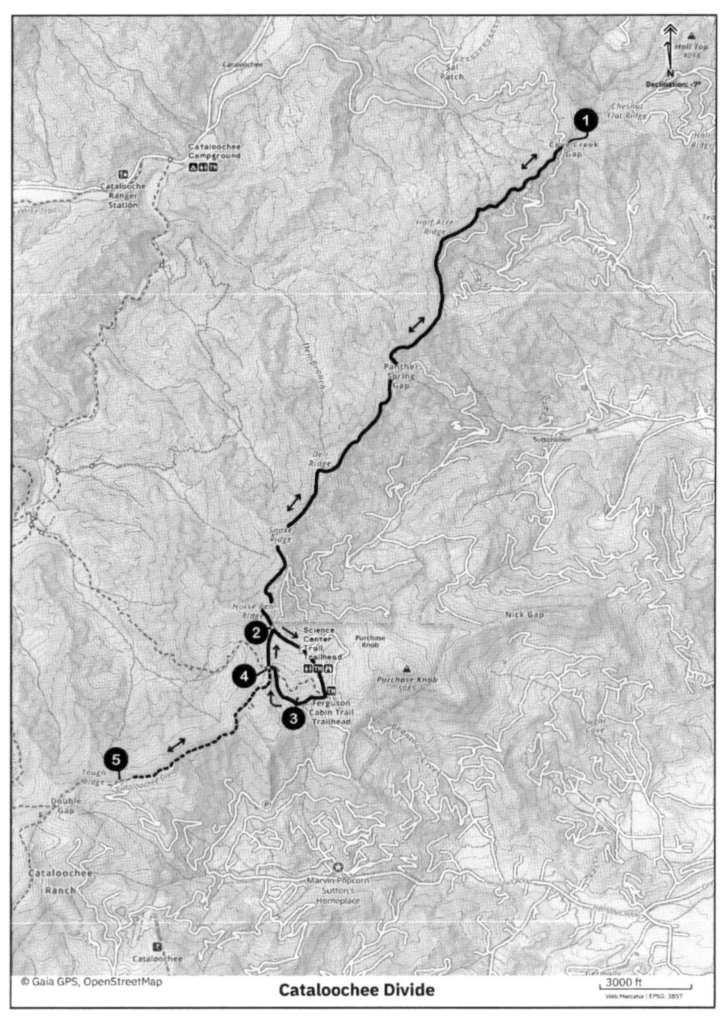

Cataloochee Divide

OVERVIEW

This hike, while longer, starts at an elevation of a tick over 4,100 feet and rolls along the ridgeline just inside the park boundary, never climbing or descending aggressively. The Cataloochee Divide Trail is one of my favorite park trails, and I've spent many an afternoon with my family on the Appalachian Highlands Science Learning Center's expansive lawn, enjoying the distant views of the Pisgah Range while eating a packed picnic lunch.

Even if you take only an out-and-back journey on the Cataloochee Divide Trail, which never wanders far from the park's boundary and is marked with a split-rail fence built in the 1930s by the Civilian Conservation Corps, it will be a day well spent in the Smokies. However, you will surely miss the most unique aspect of the adventure if you neglect to add the loop portion to this lollipop-style route. Take the time to venture to the Appalachian Highlands Science Learning Center and Ferguson Cabin, both of which were included in the largest land donation the park has ever received from a family.

This trail boasts treasures in every season: spring wildflowers, a variety of fungi in summer, colorful fall foliage and open views through the trees in winter. This hike holds a very special place in my heart, and I hope it will come to hold a space in yours, too.

THE STATS

Distance: 11-mile "lollipop" loop; extending the hike to include a visit to The Swag adds 2 miles
Difficulty: Difficult (due to the length of hike, but the trail is less challenging than most hikes in the Smokies.)
Elevation Gain and Loss: 1,581-foot gain, 1,585-foot loss
Maps: National Geographic no. 229 Great Smoky Mountains National Park; USGS 7.5' Cove Creek Gap, Dellwood
Trailhead GPS Coordinates: 35.63260, -83.04499
Highlights: Outstanding view of Cold Mountain and Mount Pisgah, high-elevation ridgeline trail, meadow walk and well-preserved homesites
Notes: A parking permit is required to park a car for more than fifteen minutes anywhere in Great Smoky Mountains National Park. Permits can be purchased online or at kiosks and visitor centers around the park. Dogs are not allowed. The learning center offers seasonal restroom facilities.

Driving Directions: From Interstate 40, take exit 20 (U.S. 276) and turn right onto Cove Creek Road. Follow it for 5.8 miles to Cove Creek Gap. There is a small parking pullout for Cataloochee Divide Trail on the left side of the road at the park boundary.

WAYPOINTS

1. Cataloochee Divide trailhead
2. unnamed trail to the Appalachian Highlands Learning Center (4.2 miles)
3. Ferguson Cabin (5.0 miles)
4. Cataloochee Divide and McKee Branch Junction (5.5 miles)
5. The Swag

HIKE DESCRIPTION

The Cataloochee Divide Trail nearly became a road in the 1970s, when a proposal was submitted to the Park Service for a "Circle the Smokies" road. Thankfully, this proposal did not come to fruition, and the only traffic you'll encounter here now are hikers and equestrians.

The hike starts with a gentle ascent from the trailhead through a grove of white pine trees (**1**). White pines are easy to distinguish from other pine species through two characteristics. First, there are five needles on each of a white pine's bundle (remembering there are also five letters in "white" is a useful mnemonic). Also, the branches of white pine grow in distinct whorls around the tree's trunk, like spokes on a wheel. Each whorl is indicative of a year's worth of growth. The trees along the trail quickly transition to predominately deciduous second-growth varieties, such as hickories, locusts, striped maples and a variety of oaks. You'll pass a few privately owned homes on the other side of the split-rail fence.

In 1.2 miles, the trail levels off temporarily. Be on the lookout for a distinct opening in the trees on the right side, framing Cataloochee Valley far below you. You won't be able to see the valley meadows through the trees, but you will be able to spot distant peaks, such as Mount Sterling, with its sixty-foot-tall steel fire tower; Noland Mountain, which divided the Big and Little Cataloochee settlements; and Scottish Mountain to the east.

Continuing down the trail in late summer and early fall, you'll likely wade between patches of white snakeroot that overlap the trail. It's easy to identify these plants with their delicate bundles of white flowers that sprout from the tops of their stalks, which can be up to three feet tall. It was believed by early European settlers that the plant could treat snakebites, hence its name. It does not, however, treat snakebites any more than trying to suck the venom from a wound.

What early settlers didn't know is that this plant contains a toxin called tremetol, and it was responsible for Nancy Lincoln's (Abraham Lincoln's mother's) death when she was only thirty-four years old. Milk sickness occurs when someone drinks milk from a cow that has grazed on snakeroot, as tremetol accumulates in the milk. Pasteurization does not kill the toxin, but modern farming practices have nearly eliminated the risk of someone contracting the illness.

Around the two-mile mark, the trail dips briefly, passes through Panther Spring Gap and then starts another gradual ascent, where it gently climbs through more second-growth forest, seasonally peppered with a variety of wildflowers. Panther Spring Gap was named for a Cataloochee folktale that involves a young girl who was dragged away screaming by a panther. The prevailing thought among scientists is that panthers have long been extirpated from this region, but unconfirmed sightings have occurred through the years.

After Panther Spring Gap, you'll generally continue following the ridgeline. In late summer, the trail can become overgrown through this lush area—thankfully with false nettle rather than wood nettle, which has "hair" on its leaves and a stem whose sting can often cause an itchy rash.

Around the three-mile mark, the trail levels briefly again, and here, you'll pass a few rock outcrops. In another quarter of a mile, the trail passes a large field on the left with an opening in the split-rail fence. There is a three-sided structure here, signed as Taylor's Turnaround, with a bench inside, but it is located on private property, and there are "No Trespassing" signs posted.

In 4.2 miles, amid a long descent lined with mountain laurel, you'll arrive at the junction with a trail that comes in from the left (**2**). A park sign will indicate it leads to the science center. Take this left turn to ascend the hill. It's a short climb, and soon, you'll level out on a broad shelf before you gently descend past a wild hog trap on the right side of the trail.

In the early 1900s, between sixty and one hundred European wild boars escaped a North Carolina hunting ranch. Over the years, they bred with local feral hogs and spread through Western North Carolina and East Tennessee. Another species of hog in the park was presumably brought from other states and released so they could be hunted. However they got here, they are unwanted visitors and are the most concerning of the nonnative species the park. Each year, usually between December and June, approximately 275 of these nonnative hogs are actively trapped and shot by the park's wildlife managers to slow down the habitat destruction and disease they spread.

After passing the trap, you'll soon emerge from the woods and on the edge of a meadow, which becomes increasingly more expansive as you continue walking the mowed path through it. You'll pass a weather monitoring station with a webcam, which you can look up on the park's website to see the view from this spot at any time. The Appalachian Highlands Science Learning Center and its parking area come into view next.

When you arrive at the learning center, take your time to look around the outside of what was once the former home of Kathryn McNeil and Voit Gilmore. Imagine what it must have been like to call this your summer residence, complete with a tennis court and swimming pool. The couple eventually divorced, but Kathryn acquired the home in the settlement. Her family continued using it, but in 2000, instead of selling the enormous property, she generously donated it to the park.

> *I love every part of it, and it comforts me as only a special place can. The Knob framed in the big window beckons to me like an old friend. "I'll be up there soon," I whisper. "Let me get my boots on first."*
>
> —*Kathryn McNeil,* Purchase Knob: Essays from a Mountain Notebook

The home, along with 535 acres of land that were contiguous with the park's boundary, represented the largest donation of acreage in the park's existence. Locally referred to as "The Purchase," a nod to the closest prominent knoll visible from the front deck or lawn, the home became "one of five initial Learning Centers created by Congress to support research in the National Parks and to transmit the information generated to the public." (Visit the N.C. Environmental Education website for more information.) Each year, the learning center hosts about five thousand students, teachers and scientists.

You may encounter researchers or school groups while you explore the grounds, but the interior of the learning center is not open to the public without an invitation. However, the park built an additional wing, which is connected to the original home by a breezeway, and it has bathrooms that are open to the public seasonally.

As you stand on the front deck of the learning center, you can see Purchase Knob front and center before you, its sloped summit leaning to the

View of the Great Balsam Range from the learning center's front porch. *Photograph by the author.*

right. Farther out, Pisgah National Forest's Great Balsam Range stretches out before you. Cold Mountain's broad summit ridge and Mount Pisgah's narrow, conical peak are the easiest to identify. On a clear day with low humidity, you can test your vision by trying to spot the transmission tower on Mount Pisgah's summit.

When you tear yourself away from this idyllic setting, you'll want to make your way down the hill that leads from the front deck and passes through the opening in the split-rail fence. The park service keeps the path through this meadow mowed, and that's what you'll want to follow. If you're there in the summer, the meadow is a visual feast, with wildflowers like wild bergamot, goldenrod, New York ironweed, bee balm, asters, daisies, coneflowers and Queen Anne's lace growing in profusion. Please be mindful of the park rules and follow "Leave No Trace" practices through this area; do not pick the flowers or traipse through them. If you come across brambles with ripe berries alongside the trail, however, it is fine to indulge in a trail snack.

Near the bottom of the meadow, you'll come to a signed intersection with a trail that bisects the meadow path. Cross through this intersection and keep walking until you reach the next trail intersection. At this junction, take a right and head down the grassy path, which dips and rises and passes a few weathered, gnarly apple trees that still produce fruit. More than thirty apple trees that are well over one hundred years in age still grow in this area. They are believed to be the oldest apple trees in any U.S. national park.

The path soon ends at the Ferguson Cabin, the highest-elevation cabin in the national park, and the nearby springhouse (**3**). The cabin is open to visitors, so look inside. On your way up the steps that lead to the cabin's front porch, look for evidence that a fox visited while the concrete was setting on one of the steps. Also, in the lawn in front of the house, there's another gnarly apple tree with evidence of a black bear's claw marks along its trunk.

This one-room cabin was built from parts of the original structure, which was built in 1874. The original home had two buildings separated by a breezeway, also known as a "dog trot." It sits on a stone foundation, unlike many of the other cabins in the Smokies, which are separated from the ground by a stack of rocks. It was built by John Love Ferguson, who purchased the land for the price of $447 and one horse. He cleared the land to raise livestock and for agricultural use. The apple trees you pass on the

The Ferguson Cabin is always a hit with children. *Photograph by the author.*

way to the cabin were known to be of the highest quality because of the conditions in which they grew at higher elevations, with cool nights and hot days during the summer.

Hugh Glenn Ferguson, one of John Ferguson's sons, who lived to be ninety-nine years old, helped pick and haul the apples to Waynesville for market. The family would carry over forty bushels per wagonload, as Ferguson conveyed in a 1999 interview.

When you're ready to leave this mountain oasis, look for the faint path that leads into the woods on the right side of the front lawn. Follow it for half a mile, mostly uphill, and a rock hop across a first order brook that feeds into Hemphill Creek far below. Then you'll come to a four-way junction of trails at around the five-and-a-half-mile mark.

Across from you will be the start of McKee Branch Trail; Cataloochee Divide Trail runs to the right and left (**4**). In another mile to the left, just over the park boundary, is The Swag, a luxurious yet cozy Relais & Chateaux inn with its own fascinating history (**5**). If you have the time and inclination, it's worth the extra two-mile round trip to enjoy the views at Gooseberry Knob, the bald knoll where the inn holds its decadent picnic lunches twice weekly.

If you'd like to skip the excursion to The Swag, turn right onto Cataloochee Divide Trail and follow it for 4.6 miles back to Cove Creek Gap and your waiting car.

THE SWAG

The founders of The Swag, Dan and Deener Matthews, originally intended to build only a private family getaway on their property, which was formerly used to grow potatoes. While camping with their children on the land, they dreamed of building an authentic log home—but one with its own built-in history. They eventually built a home on the high ridge. The oldest timbers used in the home came from Lonesome Valley Primitive Baptist Church in Tennessee and dated to 1785.

In 1982, the World's Fair was held in Knoxville, Tennessee, and the organizers asked the Matthews family if they would be willing to open their home for paying guests. They graciously agreed to the request. The guests they took in, however, were so enamored with the setting and the home that they never made it to the World's Fair. When they asked to book a stay the following year, Deener decided to become an innkeeper, while Dan continued his career as an Episcopal priest.

The name they chose for the inn originates from the Appalachian name of the geographical feature where the property sits—a *swag*—a dip between two mountain peaks that is not deep enough to be considered a gap or pass. The Swag's reputation for excellence and hospitality grew quickly. The Matthewses welcomed guests as if they were family members coming to visit, and a sense of community and fellowship followed, especially among repeat guests.

In 2018, the Matthewses retired, and The Swag was purchased by a Knoxville-based couple, Annie and David Colquitt, who had honeymooned at the inn. Annie's family had longstanding connections with the Matthewses, so she and David understood the special legacy they were inheriting with the purchase.

The Colquitts have only enhanced the beauty and charm of the property since becoming its guardians, including adding dining capacity to accommodate nonlodging guests for dinner or Sunday brunch and for picnics on Gooseberry Knob. It's an unforgettable place to spend a special occasion, whether you come for a meal and to enjoy the grounds or stay for a night or two. You'll likely agree with a former inn brochure that it's a place "where the busy world is hushed and the fever of life is distant."

CONTINUING EDUCATION

McNeil, Kathryn. *Purchase Knob: Essays from a Mountain Notebook.* Fifthian Press, 1999.

6
LAKESHORE TRAIL AND FONTANA DAM

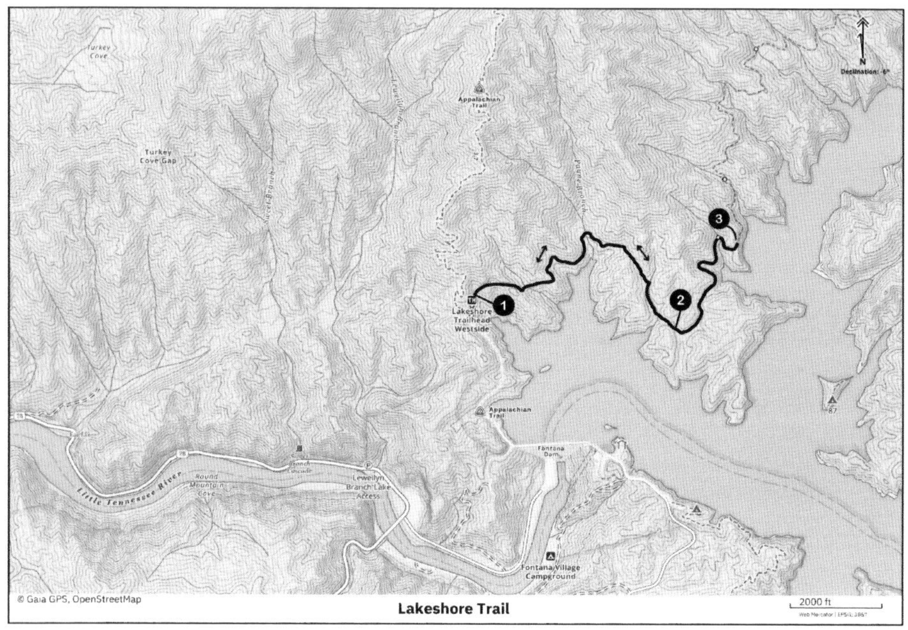

Lakeshore Trail

OVERVIEW

Lakeshore Trail, the second-longest trail in Great Smoky Mountains National Park, extends thirty-five miles from Fontana Dam to its end at the "Road to Nowhere," near Bryson City. This hike will cover only a small portion of its length, but it's a walk through time, rich in history. Reserve some time before or after your hike to explore the Fontana Dam area. There is a visitor center at the dam (which even has showers available to the public in the bathrooms), but it is open only seasonally.

THE STATS

Distance: 5.0 miles (11.5-mile loop option)
Difficulty: Easy (the loop option is Most Difficult)
Elevation Gain and Loss: 235-foot gain, 235-foot loss
Maps: National Geographic no. 229 Great Smoky Mountains National Park; USGS 7.5' Fontana Dam
Trailhead GPS Coordinates: 35.46043, -83.81107
Highlights: Fontana Dam (check the Tennessee Valley Authority's website for the visitor center's operating hours); numerous historical artifacts along the trail, including World War II–era automobiles
Notes: This hike can be combined with the Shuckstack Lookout Tower hike (chapter 2), creating an eleven-and-a-half-mile loop. A parking permit is required to park a car for more than fifteen minutes anywhere in Great Smoky Mountains National Park. Permits can be purchased online or at kiosks and visitor centers around the park. Dogs are not allowed. The Fontana Dam Visitor Center is open seasonally; check the Tennessee Valley Authority's website for its operating hours.
Driving Directions: From Bryson City, go west on NC 74 toward Murphy, North Carolina. In 8.3 miles, turn right on N.C. Highway 28. Go north 21.3 miles and turn right on County Road 1245 (Fontana Dam Road). Continue about 1.3 miles to the dam. Drive across the dam and bear right at the fork, just past the dam. Dead end into the parking area about 0.6 miles from the dam.

WAYPOINTS

1. trailhead
2. abandoned automobile and homestead (1.5 miles)
3. Nantahala Formation rocks (2.2 miles)

HIKE DESCRIPTION

Lakeshore Trail is frequently used by hikers at both ends of its east–west route. However, relative to the other 801 miles of trails in the 522,427-acre national park, it offers much more solitude, especially on this western end.

The hike starts at the back of the parking area, and the trail begins as a degraded roadbed that was once NC Highway 288 (**1**).

After the creation of Fontana Dam, the flow of the Little Tennessee River was impeded, and Fontana Lake was formed as a result. The lake submerged sections of the highway, closing it to vehicular traffic; however, eliminating this thoroughfare proved to be a minor setback in comparison to the rest of the challenges it presented. The dam and lake now collectively occupied 67,800 acres, and over 600 families had to move before the lake water covered their homes. In addition, more than one thousand graves had to be reinterred in a different location.

In 0.3 miles, the trail leaves the roadbed, leading you to a single-track trail. The Whiting Manufacturing Company had stripped this area clean of hardwoods by the late 1920s, but it has recovered well, with a variety of oaks—white, red and chestnut—standing tall around you. However, they are not so dense as to obscure your view of the lake from time to time.

The trail descends into a small drainage, crossing Payne Branch at the 0.8-mile mark. This branch was named for the Payne family, who settled in this area in the 1880s. Daniel Payne and his oldest son, Marcus, worked as loggers. The elder Payne saved enough of his income to purchase a Model-T Ford and a Victrola record player, and community members accused the Paynes of getting "bigity" with such luxuries.

The trail meanders along, clinging to the finger contours of Shuckstack Mountain, climbing for a short period up and over one of its ridges. It then rejoins the NC Highway 288 roadbed for another half mile. Notice the impressive rock walls on the left side of the trail.

At the one-and-a-half-mile mark, start looking for automobiles and an old homestead marked by a grove of black walnut trees and four shrubs that form a ninety-degree corner (**2**). In addition to their walnuts that provided sustenance to settlers, black walnut trees had practical uses, such as the creation of dye. A few hundred yards farther, another automobile, nearly buried in the earth, can be seen beside a double-trunk sycamore tree. A faint, unpaved roadbed is just to the right in this area, but go left to continue down the remains of NC 288. At this junction, the remnants of a rock retaining wall can be seen to the left and down the slope.

Continue down the old NC 288 roadbed, and you'll soon come across four more hulls of 1930s-era automobiles to the side of the trail, one of which is upside down. During World War II, tires for civilians were in short supply, since so many were needed for the war effort. These cars were likely abandoned when their tires wore out, even if they were in good running

Abandoned car on Lakeshore Trail. *Photograph by the author.*

order. Fontana Lake's rising waters and the subsequent submerging of parts of NC Highway 288 likely also played a factor in their abandonment.

At 2.2 miles, an interesting conglomeration of minerals—slate, mica and schist—comprise the impressive outcroppings of Nantahala Formation rock to the left of the trail (**3**). After the logging companies stripped this area clean of trees by the late 1920s, Fontana Mining Company set up shop, operating a mine nearby. Over the next seventeen years, more than 1,000 pounds of high-grade copper was extracted, as were 250 pounds of gold and 14,500 pounds of silver.

Continue another 0.3 miles until you reach an area where the trail forks. Route 288 continues to the right, and Lakeshore Trail heads off to the left. Unless you wish to travel farther for the sake of seeing what you can see, it's time to retrace your steps back to your car (with tires) 2.5 miles away. If you were to walk the length of Lakeshore Trail, it would end at the tunnel where Lakeview Drive, otherwise known as the "Road to Nowhere," ends (chapter 3 details its history).

FONTANA DAM

Fontana Lake, 29 miles long, encompassing 10,320 acres, is a sight to behold from high above in Great Smoky Mountains National Park. At 480 feet tall, Fontana Dam holds the accolade of being the tallest dam east of the Rockies. Its construction was completed by 1944, after five thousand laborers, working shifts around the clock, seven days a week, built it at breakneck speed in thirty-six months.

The dam was authorized by Congress nine days after the attack on Pearl Harbor in response to a need for extra electricity to ramp up the production of aluminum. Extra power was needed to support Oak Ridge National Laboratory's nuclear research and its involvement with the Manhattan Project, the top-secret mission that produced the world's first nuclear weapons and helped end World War II. Once built, the dam held back the Little Tennessee River and created Fontana Lake. Since Fontana wasn't designed as an overflow dam, water does not spill over its top but is released into the river through spillways channeled through the dam's base.

The Fontana Village area, a small tourist-driven community near the dam, housed the five thousand people who built the dam. Nowadays, the resort is a popular stop for Appalachian Trail thru hikers who wish to take a night off the trail and sleep in a bed rather than a shelter or tent.

For thru hikers who'd rather stay on the trail, the "Fontana Hilton" shelter, located 0.4 miles south of the dam's visitor center, is the next best thing. The Hilton corporation might take offense to the comparison though, since nothing about this humble dwelling resembles a Hilton-branded hotel. But to a thru hiker looking for a place to rest their weary head, it is considered one of the most desirable of the 250 shelters that dot the nearly 2,200-mile-long footpath, thanks to its lakefront view, restrooms (with showers, even) and increased capacity for hikers. No reservations or fees are required to stay in the shelter, and it's worth a side trip to peek in when you're visiting the dam. The Appalachian Trail continues past the shelter and crosses the bridge over the 2,365-foot-wide dam.

Opposite: World War II poster. *National Archives and Records Administration.*

Above: Fontana Dam, with Shuckstack Mountain in the background. *Jill Lang.*

The movie *Nell* (1994) was partially filmed on Fontana Lake. Nell's cabin was built for the film in one of the lake's secluded coves. It remained in place for several years after filming, but as it was part of a movie set and not designed to withstand time or the elements, it was eventually removed.

Many people mistakenly believe the famous scene of Harrison Ford's character jumping from the top of a dam to escape capture in *The Fugitive* (1993) was filmed at Fontana Dam; however, this scene was filmed at nearby Cheoah Dam.

CONTINUING EDUCATION

Nell. Polygram Filmed Entertainment and Egg Pictures, 1994.

7
LITTLE CATALOOCHEE TRAIL

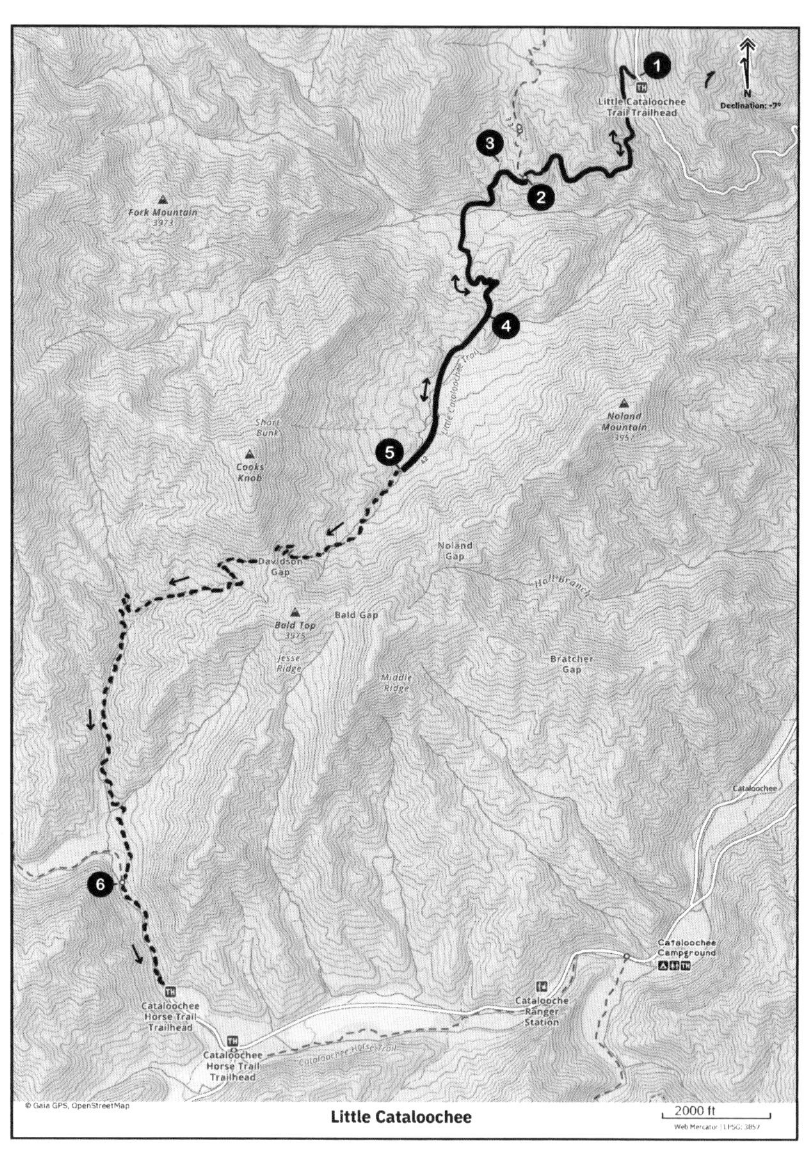

OVERVIEW

Before Great Smoky Mountains National Park existed, the Cataloochee area was home to more residents than any other location within the park's boundaries. The combined Cataloochee communities, including the Big Cataloochee, Little Cataloochee and Caldwell Fork communities, boasted 1,251 residents at their peak in 1910.

Nowadays, you'll likely encounter only a handful of fellow hikers on the peaceful Little Cataloochee Trail. This hike will lead you to three of the most well-preserved historical structures on the North Carolina side of the park, and it's an educational and entertaining route to explore with children. After the hike, it's worth your while to drive to Cataloochee Valley and visit the historical structures there, too. If you're in the valley around sunrise or sunset, you'll likely see elk, which were reintroduced to the park in 2001 (see chapter 5 for the history of the elk reintroduction).

You can also complete this hike as a one-way shuttle, totaling 6.2 miles, and the directions for this hike are included at the end of this chapter.

THE STATS

Distance: 5.2 miles (5.6 miles with a side trip to the Hannah Cemetery)
Difficulty: Moderate
Elevation Gain and Loss: 781-foot gain, 781-foot loss
Maps: USGS 7.5' Cove Creek Gap; National Geographic no. 229 Great Smoky Mountains National Park
Trailhead GPS Coordinates: 35.67614, -83.08726
Highlights: Smokies history and historical structures, possible wildlife sightings, spring wildflowers
Notes: A parking permit is required to park a car for more than fifteen minutes anywhere in Great Smoky Mountains National Park. Permits can be purchased online or at kiosks and visitor centers around the park. Check for road closures in the Cataloochee Valley area during the winter. Dogs are not allowed on this trail.
Driving Directions: From Interstate 40, take exit 20 (U.S. 276) and turn right onto Cove Creek Road. Then follow the road up and over Cove Creek Gap and into Great Smoky Mountains National Park. In 7.3 miles, you'll come to an intersection where the gravel road meets a paved road to the left, which leads into Cataloochee Valley. Cross over the paved road

to continue on unpaved Route 284. Follow this road for 2.1 miles and turn right where the road splits toward Big Creek and Cosby. In 3.5 miles, Little Cataloochee Trailhead is located on the left side of the road with a small pullout for cars on the right.

WAYPOINTS

1. Little Cataloochee Trail trailhead
2. intersection with Long Bunk Trail (1 mile)
3. John Jackson Hannah cabin (1.3 miles)
4. Little Cataloochee Baptist Church (2 miles)
5. Cook cabin (2.6 miles)
6. intersection with Pretty Hollow Gap Trail on the one-way shuttle hike option (5.3 miles)

HIKE DESCRIPTION

This delightful hike starts at the trailhead on Route 284, an unpaved road that's as much of an adventure as the hike itself, winding close to the park's border. **(1)** Little Cataloochee Trail starts just beyond the trail sign and a gate that extends across the trail. The trail itself is a roadbed that initially dips down a short hill into a mature forest.

Ethnologist James Mooney noted that Gadalutsi, the Cherokee term for this area, translates to "standing in a row." The prevailing thoughts are that the Cherokee were describing the tall mountains that frame the area or perhaps referring to the tall peaks of the Fraser firs and red spruces that line the ridgelines above the basin. The Cherokee did not inhabit this remote area, although they did hunt in it.

Two distinct settlements occupied the area: Cataloochee Valley, or Big Cataloochee; and Little Cataloochee, which is your destination on this hike. The two settlements were divided by Noland Mountain, named for William and Elizabeth Hannah Noland, who became the first permanent residents of Cataloochee after William returned from a hunting trip in the area in 1839. It wasn't until between 1854 and 1860 that the offspring of the original settlers of Cataloochee Valley spread their wings and began calling Little Cataloochee home. To visit either neighboring community, residents had to travel over Davidson Gap, between Bald Top and Cooks Knob.

Well, it was quite a chore to go through Davidson Gap....It would take more than a day to go over to Little Cataloochee and back....So, in one respect, it was separated about as much as New York City and California are today (by airplane).

—*Raymond Caldwell,*
Cataloochee: Lost Settlement of the Smokies

In 0.3 miles, cross the bridge that spans Correll Branch, and you'll start to climb on the other side. In one mile, you'll reach the intersection with Long Bunk Trail (**2**). If time allows, consider making the 0.2-mile side trip up this trail to visit the Hannah Cemetery. The fenced cemetery holds around fifty graves, including those of veterans of the Spanish-American War and World War II and John Jackson and Martha Ann Hannah, whose restored cabin you can visit on this hike.

As you continue down Little Cataloochee Trail, beyond the Long Bunk Trail junction, look for a side trail to the right after you travel another 0.2 miles. A couple hundred feet up this steep path sits the one-room cabin of John Jackson and Martha Hannah that was built in 1864 (**3**). The land above the cabin was used for farming by Mr. Hannah, and the family's nearby apple orchard purportedly contained one of the world's largest apple trees.

Hannah Cabin on Little Cataloochee Trail. *Photograph by the author.*

The Hannahs' son Mack was one of the most successful apple growers in this region. James, another of the Hannahs' sons, was also no stranger to hard work, as he carried the mail between Big and Little Cataloochee.

The National Park Service restored this cabin in 1976, using period tools, such as broad axes and foot adzes. Many of the original bricks, created from local clay, were used for the fireplace's restoration. The broad puncheon floor of the cabin, with planks nearly two and a half feet wide, is particularly impressive.

Retrace your steps on the side trail that leads to the Hannah cabin and turn right to rejoin the Little Cataloochee Trail. Soon, you'll pass through what used to be the thriving commercial hub of Little Cataloochee: Ola, named after residents Will and Rachel Messer's daughter Viola, who was one of their eleven children. Ola had many commercial buildings, including a general store, post office, blacksmith shop and gristmill.

About 0.7 miles from the Hannah cabin, you'll arrive at Little Cataloochee Baptist Church, perched above the trail on a small knoll with a flat shelf (**4**). The white-painted church with scalloped eaves is arguably one of the most picturesque historical structures in the park. The interior is just as charming as the exterior, with white walls and wooden pews encircling a simple pulpit with a wood stove in front of it.

The quaint church was built in 1889 by local residents, including Will Messer, who built the steeple and pulpit. Other residents helped foot the cost of construction. William J. Hannah donated the four-hundred-pound bell, which still resides in the prominent belfry. When anyone died in Little Cataloochee, the bell was rung, and the number of peals corresponded to the person's age when they died, according to Mark Hannah, who held the unique distinction of being a Cataloochee native and then, later, a park ranger for more than thirty years. Once or twice a month, circuit riders from Waynesville visited the church in exchange for a five- to ten-dollar donation from the collection plate.

> *During these services there is a good deal of running in and out by the men and boys, most of whom gradually congregate on the outside to whittle, gossip, drive bargains, and debate among themselves some point of dogma that is too good to keep still about.*
>
> —*Horace Kephart*

The building was also used as a schoolhouse until two others were built elsewhere in the community. Children were sent to school with woven lunch

Little Cataloochee Baptist Church. *Photograph by the author.*

baskets filled with anything from biscuits and molasses to fresh vegetables grown by their families. Occasionally, a piece of ham or a slice of fruit pie was included as a special treat. Interestingly, only one wedding was ever held in the church—that of Flora Messer to Charles Morrow. Most weddings during that time took place in homes, before the hearth.

In front of the church, down a small hill, is a small cemetery with around sixty former congregants buried in it. Notice the young ages on many of the headstones, such as that of Lennis Mae Morrow, the daughter of Flora and Charles Morrow, who were married in the church. Lennis Mae's date of birth and death are the same, with her headstone reading, "only a bud to bloom in Heaven." Leola Messer, the daughter of W.M. and Myrtle Messer, has the same inscription and also bears a single date for her birth and death—a sobering reminder of the challenges families faced here in the early twentieth century, including the influenza epidemic.

After you've explored the church and its surroundings, return to the trail and turn left. Walk for another 0.6 miles alongside Coggins Branch until you reach the Daniel J. Cook cabin to the right of the trail (**5**). This one-room log cabin with a loft was finished in 1856 and served as the home for Dan and Harriett Cook for more than fifty years. The cabin was dismantled, and its components were safely stored by the National Park Service in the 1970s, after it was vandalized. It was reconstructed in 1999, with another round of restoration occurring in 2017 by Asheville-based contractor The Hands of Sean Perry, which donated labor for the cause.

Dan Cook was a master carpenter, and he built much of the furniture that was used in the home, including a cherrywood corner cabinet that was embellished with a star and moon motif. Harriet made most of the family's clothes from flax she grew and wove into cloth. Even the family's shoes were made by Dan.

Across the trail from the Cook cabin, near the horse-hitching post, are the stone remains of a two-story apple house that was built by Will Messer in 1915. The walls were nearly two and a half feet thick and were constructed of stone and wood. The structure served as a storehouse for the community, as many grew apples in the favorable conditions of this region. Red and golden delicious, winesap and Stamen apples were popular varieties found in Cataloochee.

Dan Cook's daughter Rachel married Will Messer, the wealthiest Cataloochee community member. Rachel and Will Messer lived in Ola, between the Hannah cabin and Little Cataloochee Baptist Church. Though it's gone now, the eleven-room Messer home was one of the finest in the community, with modern luxuries such as acetylene lighting and hot and cold running water.

Will Messer was also the first resident of Cataloochee to own a car, but he was best known for his magnanimous gestures. Referred to as "generous, helpful and honest," he built and sold cherrywood coffins for seven dollars but donated them to families who couldn't afford the fee. He also extended credit from his general store to those who needed it, and he accepted honey, butter, nuts and berries in exchange for goods in his store, such as sugar, coffee, salt, tools and toys.

When you're ready to move on from Cook cabin, return to the Little Cataloochee Trail and retrace your steps for 2.6 miles to reach the Little Cataloochee Trail trailhead.

ONE-WAY SHUTTLE HIKE OPTION

This hike also works well as a one-way shuttle hike. Leave your car at the Pretty Hollow Gap trailhead in Cataloochee Valley and then drive a second car to the Little Cataloochee Trail trailhead on Route 284. For this route, instead of turning around at the Dan Cook Cabin, continue on Little Cataloochee Trail for 2 more miles. Climb up and over Davidson Gap until you reach the point where the trail intersects the Pretty Hollow Gap Trail at mile 5.3 (**6**). Turn left and follow Pretty Hollow Gap Trail for 0.8 miles to reach the trailhead and your waiting car.

8

OCONALUFTEE RIVER TRAIL

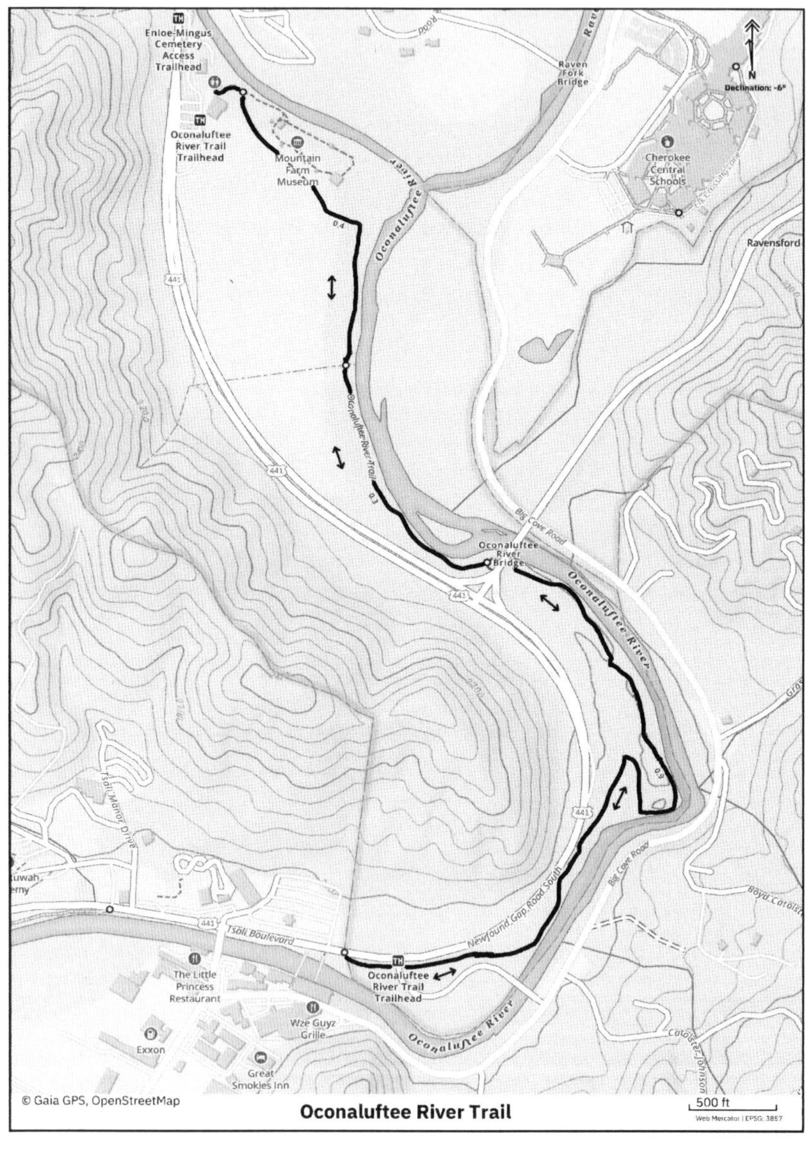

OVERVIEW

Derived from the Cherokee word egwanulti, meaning "by the river," Oconaluftee refers to one of the oldest Cherokee villages that once thrived along the river's banks. Hiking the Oconaluftee River Trail will add only about three easy trail miles of wear to your shoes, but plan on spending a lot of time in the area—more than what it takes to walk it.

The Mountain Farm Museum, located at the start of the hike, is a fantastic way to learn about the history of these mountains from the nineteenth century. The trail, meanwhile, will educate you about the former inhabitants of this land: the Cherokee. If you're lucky, you may even spot an elk or two in the meadows beside the trail, along its wooded edge or even in the river itself.

Before you start hiking, be sure to pick up the farm museum's self-guided tour booklet in the visitor center. While you're inside, spend a little time checking out the interesting exhibits on display and consider supporting the park by making a purchase in the gift shop and bookstore run by Smokies Life.

THE STATS

Distance: 3.2 miles, out and back
Difficulty: Easy
Elevation Gain and Loss: 55-foot gain, 55-foot loss
Maps: USGS 7.5' Smokemont, National Geographic no. 229 Great Smoky Mountains National Park
Trailhead GPS Coordinates: 35.51272, -83.30624
Highlights: Engaging outdoor museum, easy riverside trail, spring wildflowers, elk sightings, family-friendly attractions
Notes: A parking permit is required to park a car for more than fifteen minutes anywhere in Great Smoky Mountains National Park. Permits can be purchased online or at kiosks and visitor centers around the park. Unique to this trail and the Gatlinburg River Trail, leashed dogs are allowed; however, they are not allowed inside the Mountain Farm Museum. Restrooms are located beside the visitor center. The trail is stroller accessible (but I recommend using a jogging stroller to best handle the terrain). Maintain a safe distance of fifty yards from elk.

Driving Directions: The Oconaluftee Visitor Center is located in Great Smoky Mountains National Park off of Newfound Gap Road (US 441), two miles north of Cherokee, North Carolina. The Mountain Farm Museum is next to the visitor center, and the Oconaluftee River Trail runs parallel to the museum.

DESCRIPTION

This riverside trail starts just before the entrance to the outdoor farm museum. Meander through the museum's exhibits, and ask if there are any ranger or volunteer-led programs that day. The expansive plot is a great place to let children run off some energy, but make sure they leave enough to keep hiking the Oconaluftee River Trail, which picks back up on the far side of the museum.

The museum's log structures include a springhouse, apple house, drover's barn and working blacksmith shop. Most everything you see was built in the late 1800s and early 1900s; the buildings were relocated from various locations in and around the park in the 1960s. The Davis house, a two-story log house that once stood near Indian Creek in the Bryson City area, was

Mountain Farm Museum, Oconaluftee Visitor Center. *Michael Shake.*

built from chestnut wood before the chestnut blight decimated the American chestnut in the 1930s and 1940s.

The trail stays close to the riverbank the entire time, and there are several user trails that take you to the water's edge. Along the way, interpretive exhibits share stories about the Cherokee's spiritual connection to the Earth, including tales of The Long Man and the creation of the world. These stories unfold beneath a canopy of hardwood trees such as red maple, yellow buckeye, beech, sycamore, dogwood and tulip poplar. Eastern hemlocks are also present near the path. In spring, wildflowers abound, and more than forty species have been identified along this route.

Eventually, the trail passes under the Blue Ridge Parkway and then parallels Newfound Gap Road before crossing Big Cove Road. After this crossing, the trail ends in another 0.1 miles in a grassy area just across from some shops in Cherokee. Retrace your steps back to the Oconaluftee Visitor Center.

QUALLA BOUNDARY OF THE EASTERN BAND OF CHEROKEE INDIANS

I encourage you to spend some time in Cherokee before or after your stroll along the Oconaluftee River Trail. This area is often referred to as the "Cherokee Reservation" by visitors; however, it is not a reservation at all but is rather a land trust held by the U.S. government, commonly referred to as The Qualla Boundary.

The Qualla Boundary, spanning over fifty-seven thousand acres, was established in 1876 through negotiations between the Cherokee Nation, William Holland Thomas and the U.S. government. In the 1840s and 1850s, following the forcible relocation of eleven thousand Cherokee people after the passage of the Indian Removal Act in 1838 and 1839 (Trail of Tears), Thomas purchased the land under his name on behalf of the Cherokee people. Early in his life, Thomas worked and lived among the Cherokee people and was a close friend of Chief Yonaguska (Drowning Bear). Unlike so many other white settlers, Thomas was respected and trusted by the Cherokee people. His help was instrumental in establishing the Qualla Boundary.

During the Trail of Tears, a small group of Cherokee people managed to stay in the region and often hid in what is now Great Smoky Mountains National Park. Their descendants make up the Eastern Band of Cherokee

A Cherokee family from an illustration in the *Great Smoky Mountains National Park Guide*, 1933. *Western Carolina University Hunter Library.*

Natives who live in the Qualla Boundary today, along with those who were granted permission to stay through the treaty established in 1819 by Chief Yonguska.

The Eastern Band is one of the three federally recognized Cherokee tribes. The Qualla Boundary includes parts of Swain and Jackson Counties, and the town of Cherokee is the principal community within the boundary. A visit to The Museum of the Cherokee Indian, which "preserves and perpetuates the history, culture and stories of the Cherokee people," is a worthwhile endeavor and the perfect complement to this hike.

CONTINUING EDUCATION

Duncan, Barbara. *Living Stories of the Cherokee.* University of North Carolina Press, 1988.

PART II

PISGAH NATIONAL FOREST

9

ART LOEB TRAIL

COLD MOUNTAIN

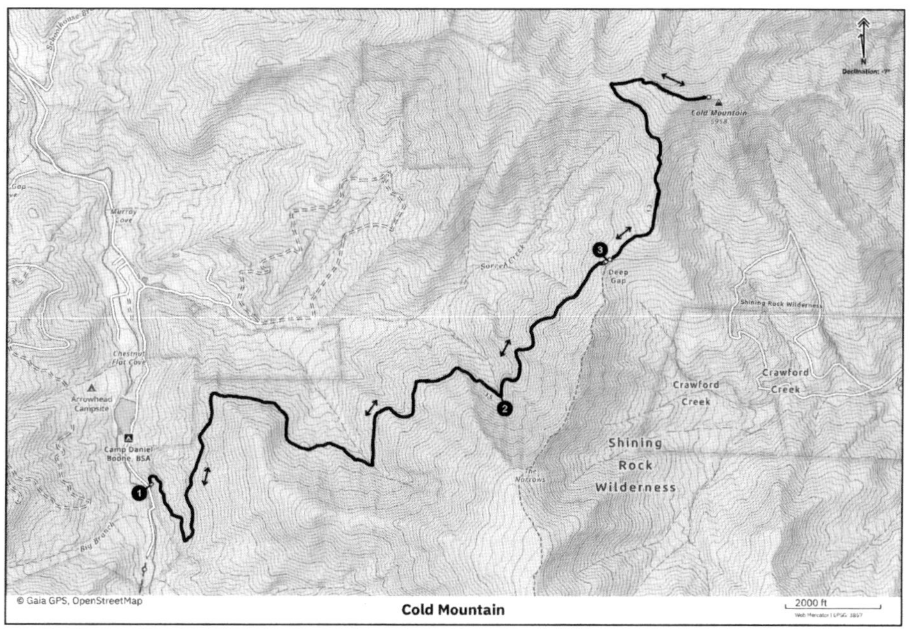

Cold Mountain

OVERVIEW

The Art Loeb Trail is a premier backpacking route in Western North Carolina, but most people who complete its thirty-mile length probably don't know much about the hiker for whom it's named. It's a shame, because his is an inspiring story and one that might provide a mental boost for hikers as they tackle its challenging terrain.

Mile for mile, the Art Loeb Trail (ALT) offers some of the most spectacular high-elevation scenery in the region. It passes over some of

Pisgah National Forest's most well-loved peaks, such as Black Balsam Knob and Tennent Mountain. This hike starts in the quiet woods near the ALT's northern terminus before it veers to reach the zenith of Cold Mountain. The mountain's broad summit is easy to spot from the Blue Ridge Parkway and other surrounding high points (notably, the Appalachian Highlands Learning Center mentioned in chapter 5), and it is one of Pisgah National Forest's crown jewels.

Cold Mountain made its mark in history when a tragic plane crash in the 1940s brought it to the attention of more than just the local hiking community. Decades later, in the 1990s, Charles Frazier's National Book Award–winning novel *Cold Mountain* brought the peak to the forefront of the public's attention yet again.

Make sure you reserve a full day for this hike. While the climb is manageable if you take your time, it's still a long one. The good news is that you'll enjoy an equally long descent on the return trip back to the trailhead.

THE STATS

Distance: 10 miles out and back
Difficulty: Most Difficult
Elevation Gain and Loss: 2,655-foot gain, 2,655-foot loss
Maps: National Geographic no. 780 Pisgah Ranger District; USGS Cruso
Trailhead GPS Coordinates: 35.38701, -82.89580
Highlights: Outstanding views of Shining Rock Wilderness, famed literary mountain, South Beyond 6,000 Challenge peak
Notes: Leashed dogs are allowed, but do not camp on the Camp Daniel Boone property.
Driving Directions: From Bethel, North Carolina, take Highway 215 South. Then turn left on State Road 1129 and continue straight until you arrive at Camp Daniel Boone. Drive slowly through the camp until you reach the large parking area just beyond the trailhead.

WAYPOINTS

1. Art Loeb Trail trailhead
2. flood-damaged area (2.8 miles)
3. Deep Gap (3.8 miles)

HIKE DESCRIPTION

This hike begins at the large stone steps on the northern edge of the large parking area beside the trailhead signboard (**1**). You'll initially hear the Little East Fork of the Pigeon River, since it runs parallel to the parking area, but the sound dissipates quickly as you ascend. The climb is steep at first, but it becomes less aggressive within a few tenths of a mile, when it begins a pattern of rising and leveling, all the way to Deep Gap, nearly four miles away.

At the one-mile mark, an old roadbed from the right merges onto and becomes the trail for a short distance before it veers to the left (you'll stay to the right). Shortly after, you'll descend a flight of wooden steps built into the hill. Look for an interesting maple on the right side of the trail, hugging the flat side of an enormous boulder.

In 1.8 miles, an obvious user trail veers downhill toward Sorrells Creek and a flat campsite, but you'll continue to the right and cross the creek using its exposed rocks. In another half mile, you'll cross another branch using the rocks.

In 2.8 miles, you'll encounter a tricky area of the trail where historic flooding and a landslide occurred in the wake of Tropical Depression Fred on August 17, 2021 (**2**). Over eight inches of rain fell within a span of about two to three hours at the headwaters of the Pigeon River in Graveyard Fields, causing massive destruction through many of its tributaries. Downstream from this site, in the small community of Cruso, six people lost their lives in this unprecedented flooding event—a tragic day for the local community.

Be cautious as you navigate your way around the remaining detritus. There is an obvious path where others have traveled, and the trail continues on the other side of the small creek, which was surely a raging torrent on that fateful day of flooding. Proceed with caution if recent storms have hit the area, and adhere to the important adage "turn around, don't drown" if the crossing appears dangerous.

Once you are on the other side of the ravine, you'll continue your climb for 3.8 miles before you reach Deep Gap, where a sign will welcome your arrival (**3**). There is a large campsite here, and it's a nice place to take a longer break before you continue your journey to Cold Mountain's summit.

When you're ready to start hiking again, look for a faint trail to the left of Deep Gap that heads gently uphill. You'll now depart the Art Loeb Trail and climb in a northbound direction on a ridge of the appropriately named Cold Mountain Trail. About midway up the climb, the trail veers left and to the west before it arrives at a piped seasonal spring on the right side of the

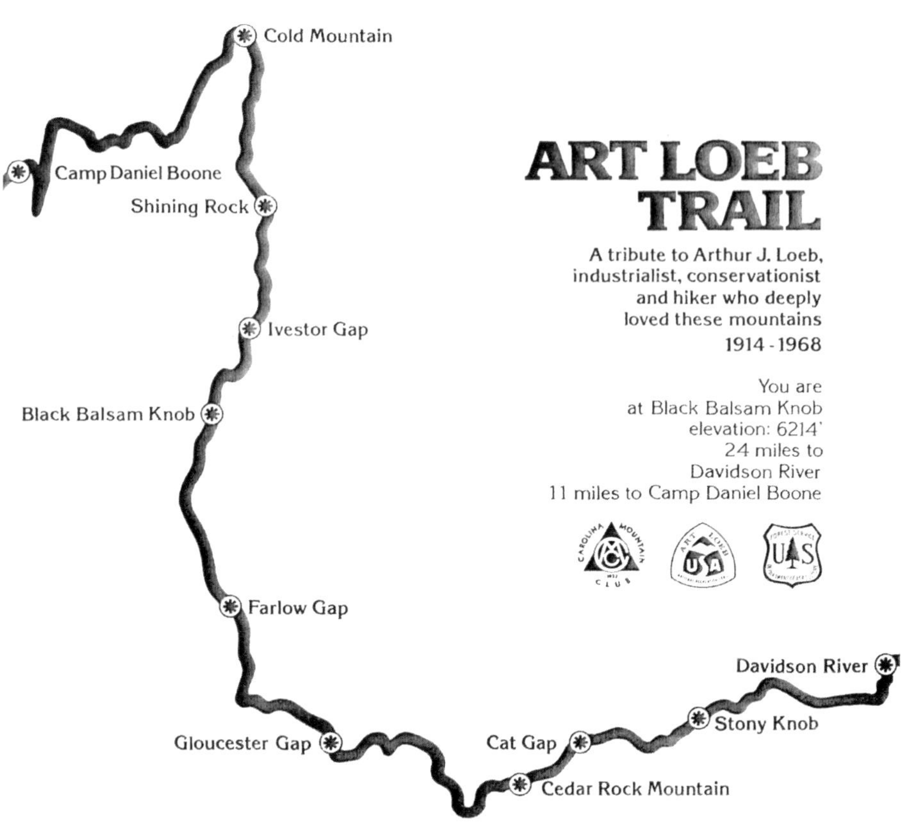

The original plaque at Black Balsam Knob (later stolen), which shows the intended path of the Art Loeb Trail over Cold Mountain, 1985. *Courtesy of the Rowell Bosse North Carolina Room, Transylvania County Library.*

trail around mile 4.4. About a tenth of a mile after the spring, the trail turns sharply east. User trails to small campsites flank the trail in multiple spots, but stay on the main path, as it winds and twists its way to the summit ridge. The foliage is dense and often obscures the trail near the actual summit, so proceed with care.

To your left, on the north side of the summit ridge, Cold Mountain has an especially sobering history. On Friday, September 13, 1946, at a home near the trailhead, Lenoir "Beanie" Moody reported he heard what he thought was an exceptionally loud clap of thunder. It caused the entire house where he was working to shake. Even the two-by-four lumber he was holding in his hand was jarred. Another nearby local heard what he assumed was a dynamite blast in the direction of Cold Mountain.

High above these men, a couple hundred feet below Cold Mountain's summit, five World War II heroes lost their lives when their U.S. Army Air Force B-25 bomber, commanded by Major General Paul Wurtsmith, crashed at a speed of about 230 miles per hour into a rock cliff on Cold Mountain's northern face. The men were returning to MacDill Air Field in Tampa from Detroit on an instrument flight plan at six thousand feet.

Records show that Wurtsmith radioed into Tri-City Airport to request a lower altitude due to poor weather and low visibility. The radio operator relayed that six thousand feet was below the safe minimum altitude for the area and asked Wurtsmith if a higher altitude was desired. He responded to inform the operator that he was now flying on CFR (contact flight), or visual control, and to request clearance to continue toward Tampa. The military report indicated the cause of the crash was "contact flight below minimum safe altitude" in bad weather, but rumors evolved. According to *Cold Mountain Bomber Crash: An Enduring Legacy*, it's rumored that a sudden downdraft forced the plane to a lower elevation, and others even believed the bomber had been "sabotaged by enemy agents in America."

The remains of the wreckage, including two engines, the fuselage and parts of the wings, were removed by helicopter in the 1980s, but much of it had been scavenged prior to that by visitors to the crash site. Shortly after the crash, a local Boy Scout troop visited the site during a navigational training exercise using a map and compass. They failed to find the site the first time, but on their second and successful trip, they tied a rope to one of the plane's propellors and slid it on dry leaves down the mountain. They mounted it upright in concrete and displayed it in the scout room of Canton's First United Methodist Church for decades before it was moved to its current home in the Canton Historical Museum.

To the right on the south face of the mountain, about 1,300 feet below the summit ridge, another aircraft tragedy claimed the lives of two civilian men in the predawn hours of May 12, 2008. A Piper PA-32-260, traveling from Rutherfordton, North Carolina, to Little Rock, Arkansas, crashed into a heavily wooded area of the mountain at an elevation of around 4,700 feet. At 10:45 p.m. the night prior, the National Weather Service had issued high-wind warnings and an airman's meteorological information AIRMET for moderate turbulence and high winds in the area. The FAA had no record of a pilot preflight weather briefing or any pilot communication with FAA facilities during the flight. The National Transportation Safety Board's report of the accident indicated that inadequate preflight planning and an

Hiker taking in the view on Cold Mountain's summit. *Melissa Coatney.*

inadvertent flight into unsafe meteorological conditions with moderate to severe turbulence contributed to the accident.

You'll know you've arrived at the highest point of the 6,030-foot peak when you find a vintage geological marker embedded in a boulder just before an opening to a small, rocky shelf on the summit ridge. Unless you encounter a hiker who is chipping away at the South Beyond 6,000 Challenge (a challenge hosted by the Carolina Mountain Club in which participants must tag the summits of forty peaks that are over 6,000 feet tall) or an ambitious Art Loeb Trail thru hiker who's opted to make a side trip to this spot, there's a good chance you'll have this space all to yourself.

The view is one of the best in the region, as the evidence of human impact on the landscape spread before you is nearly nonexistent. The Art Loeb Trail continues traveling the ridge perpendicular to where you stand and eventually crosses Tennent Mountain and Black Balsam Knob before it bisects the Blue Ridge Parkway and heads toward Pilot Mountain. The bald face of Looking Glass Rock peeks out on the left, and Mount Hardy, Sam's Knob and Little Sam's Knob are recognizable peaks to your right.

In 1997, the mountain's popularity increased again after Asheville native Charles Frazier published his award-winning novel *Cold Mountain.* In 2003, the mountain received another bump in attention when the movie adaptation of the book was released. The film received seven Oscar nominations, with an award going to Renée Zellweger for best supporting actress. Both the book and movie are worthy of your time, but as is the case with most movie adaptations, I feel the book is superior. Anyone who watched the movie and then hiked Cold Mountain was mistaken if they thought they were visiting the area where filming occurred, however. It was less expensive to film the movie in the Carpathian Mountains of Romania apparently.

When you're ready, retrace your route back to the trailhead, which sits 2,600 feet below you. After hiking to this special summit, you'll likely agree with Frazier's sentiment in *Cold Mountain*: "The mountains were our refuge, a sanctuary from the chaos of the world, offering shelter and solace."

ART LOEB: AN UNEXPECTED INSPIRATION

Arthur J. Loeb didn't start his life in the mountains of Western North Carolina, but his legacy left a lasting impact for future generations to enjoy. After graduating from Yale in 1936, he moved to Brevard to work for Ecusta Paper Mill, which was started by his cousin. The demands of his career as the company's general manager and raising his family caught up with him when he was in his mid-forties, and he suffered a heart attack. Luckily, he survived the cardiac event.

Instead of reverting back to old habits, he followed his doctor's orders and took up a new hobby: walking. Initially, walks around Brevard College's track and Lake Strauss were all he was capable of; however, he worked up to walking in the woods. With his recognizable hiking stick made from Carolina silverbell, he became an avid and experienced hiker, well known in the Carolina Mountain Club (CMC) community. He was passionate about linking existing trails to longer routes, and he discovered a way to connect trails all the way from Davidson River Campground in Brevard to Daniel Boone Boy Scout Camp in Haywood County.

Despite Loeb's dedication to a healthier lifestyle after his heart attack, he passed away from a brain tumor in 1968, when he was fifty-four years old. The CMC picked up where he left off and worked with the U.S. Forest Service and Western North Carolina Congressman Roy Taylor to establish a new thirty-mile trail in his memory.

On November 9, 1969, the Art Loeb Trail was dedicated in front of hundreds of people who attended the ceremony at the trail's northern

Art Loeb on Shining Rock in Pisgah National Forest. *Courtesy of the Rowell Bosse North Carolina Room, Transylvania County Library.*

terminus. Before the ceremony started, about two dozen friends and family walked in Art's honor from the John Rock Fish Station (which is now a state fish hatchery) to the ceremony. A wooden plaque placed at the trailhead reads, "The Art Loeb Trail, named in tribute to Arthur J. Loeb, industrialist, conservationist, and hiker, who so deeply loved these mountains."

CONTINUING EDUCATION

Canon, Doris Rollins. *Cold Mountain Bomber Crash: The Enduring Legacy.* Edwards Brothers Inc., 2005.

Frazier, Charles. *Cold Mountain.* Grove Press, 1997.

10

BUCK SPRINGS LODGE, MOUNT PISGAH

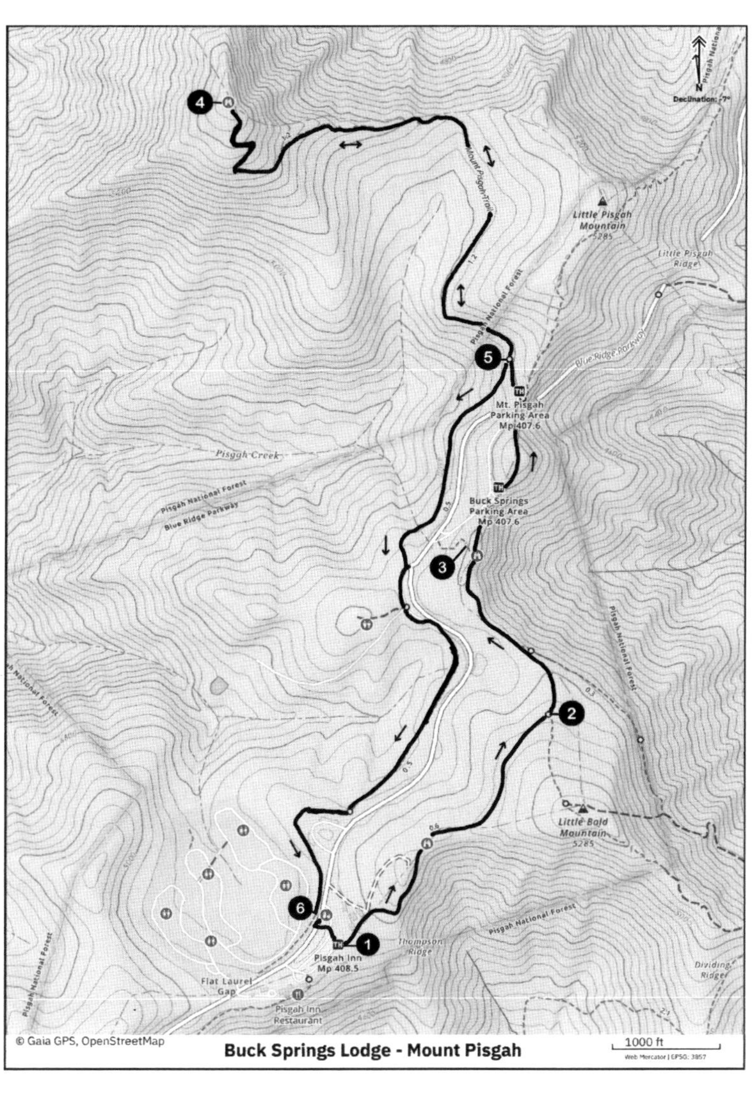

OVERVIEW

A great hike for a warm summer's day, this route passes by the remains of the former Buck Springs Lodge, George W. Vanderbilt's hunting cabin, before it heads to the pyramidal summit of Mount Pisgah (5,722 feet), which the Vanderbilt family also owned before it was sold to the U.S. Forest Service. There's a TV broadcast antenna at the top, and it makes this peak easily recognizable from the lower elevations of seven surrounding counties; however, you'll be too impressed by the panoramic views from the viewing deck to mind it much.

To better your chance of catching the widest views, check the Pisgah Lodge webcam online before you head out to make sure the area isn't overcast or suspended in a cloud. Aside from Mount Pisgah's summit, this high-elevation hike boasts mild elevation gain and loss, making it a favorable option for families and less-experienced hikers.

THE STATS

Distance: 5.2 miles
Difficulty: Moderate
Elevation Gain and Loss: 917-foot gain, 927-foot loss
Maps: National Geographic no. 780 Pisgah National Forest, Pisgah Ranger District; USGS 7.5' Cruso NC
Trailhead GPS Coordinates: 35.40329, -82.75349
Highlights: Panoramic views, Vanderbilt hunting lodge and ruins, historic Pisgah Inn, fall colors
Notes: Restrooms are available in Pisgah Inn and at the small convenience store on the north side of the inn's large parking area. Leashed dogs are allowed. This is a kid-friendly hike, but do not allow them to climb the transmission tower on Mount Pisgah. Check for closures on the Blue Ridge Parkway before setting out.
Driving Directions: From Asheville, take the Blue Ridge Parkway south for fifteen miles. The Pisgah Inn and the trailhead parking lot are between mile markers 408 and 409 on the left. Do not park in the spaces at the small country store near the inn.

WAYPOINTS

1. Pisgah Inn trailhead
2. Little Bald summit turnoff (0.7 mile)
3. site of Buck Springs Lodge (1.0 mile)
4. Mount Pisgah summit (1.5 miles)
5. signed junction (3.75 miles)
6. stairs that lead to the Blue Ridge Parkway crossing (5.1 miles)

HIKE DESCRIPTION

The hike starts on the stone steps behind the trailhead at the north end of Pisgah Inn's parking area on the Buck Spring Trail. **(1)** North Carolina's longest trail, the Mountains to Sea Trail, piggybacks onto it before continuing its 1,175-mile journey east, ending at the Outer Banks. You'll start a gentle ascent, passing humble housing for the inn's staff on the left and numbered signposts along the trail that once corresponded to an informational brochure that is no longer in print.

At 0.7 miles, you'll pass the signed junction for Little Bald's summit (a worthwhile out-and-back short side trip) **(2)** and then the Laurel Mountain Trail junction shortly thereafter. The rhododendron tunnel you'll pass through next makes for an interesting photo opportunity. If you're hiking the trail in late spring or early summer, you may even catch these trees in bloom.

One mile into your hike, begin looking for stone foundations near the trail, evidence of the former Buck Springs Lodge **(3)**. You'll soon arrive at a clearing where a bench facing east awaits you. The lodge was built in 1895 by the same architects who built the famed Biltmore Estate, located some twenty-two miles below you via the Shut-In Ridge Trail. Vanderbilt and his guests used the Shut-In Trail to access the lodge, which included the main building as well as a stable, garage and honeymoon cottage. A child's playhouse was also built for George and Edith Vanderbilt's daughter, Cornelia, to entice her to make the long journey from the valley. Although this was considered a less-opulent dwelling for the wealthy family, Buck Springs Lodge was hardly "rustic" for its time. Modern conveniences, such as hot water and electricity, were not overlooked, and there was even a year-round caretaker and seasonal staff to tend to the family and their visiting guests.

A hiker walking through a mountain laurel tunnel. *Photograph by the author.*

The National Park Service purchased the property and surrounding four hundred acres for the Blue Ridge Parkway after Edith died in 1957. The lodge was deconstructed, and all that remains now are its stone foundations and a springhouse. It's worth taking the short side trip to the picturesque springhouse. It can be accessed from the side trail that leads away from a grassy area behind the informational sign that is near the bench.

After you've explored the lodge's former site, continue north for 0.2 miles, and you'll arrive at the Buck Springs Gap parking area. If the weather is clear, you can't miss Mount Pisgah rising above you on the left as you walk across the parking area. On the opposite side of the parking area, pick up the Mountains to Sea Trail again on a short flight of stone steps that ascends to a small knoll before it descends on rocky terrain to the Mount Pisgah parking area in 0.2 miles.

Cross this parking area and look for the Mount Pisgah Trail on the far side, where you'll continue. You'll leave the Mountains to Sea Trail, which continues from the south side of the parking area. Between here and the summit, you have 712 feet to climb, but it is mostly gentle until the last 0.2 miles, where it pitches upward steeply. Soon after you start the Mount

Buck Springs Lodge. *National Park Service.*

Pisgah Trail, you'll be walking on the ground above one of the Blue Ridge Parkway's iconic tunnels, but it's unlikely you'll realize this with the woods surrounding you.

When you arrive at Mount Pisgah's summit (**4**), which was named for the biblical mountain from which Moses first saw the promised land, find a spot on the wooden observation deck to take in the sweeping scene. The 339-foot-tall WLOS ("Wonderful Land of Sky") transmission tower only obscures your views to the north; however, you'll be able to spot downtown Asheville to the northeast and the Great Craggy and Black Mountain Ranges behind it.

The Great Balsam Mountain Range runs from the southwest to the west. Due west, Cold Mountain's conical peak is easily recognizable and separated from where you stand by the East Fork of the Pigeon River. To the south, Fryingpan Mountain and its communications and lookout towers can be spotted, along with Looking Glass Rock. To the east, on a clear day, you'll be able to see all the way to the Piedmont region of the state and possibly even the Biltmore Estate, the Vanderbilt family's opulent home.

The Cherokee name for this peak is Elseetoss, but its English name dates to the early 1800s, stemming from the name of the biblical mountain from which Moses first viewed the promised land. You'll feel as if you're having a similar experience at its high-elevation summit.

Once you've taken in your fill of the view, descend the way you climbed it until you approach the Mount Pisgah parking area, about 3.75 miles into the hike. Look for the signed junction on the right, which heads toward the picnic area, campground and Frying Pan Tower (**5**). Take this trail and follow it for 1.2 miles until you reach a junction with a small flight of stairs to the left of the trail that crosses over the Blue Ridge Parkway and back to the Pisgah Inn parking area (**6**). Along this stretch, you'll pass through a parking area that has a short trail that heads to the picnic area; stop here if you'd like to explore it and have a snack before continuing. Once you arrive at the inn, you can either head out or do what I like to do and purchase a cold beverage from either the country store or Pisgah Inn's snack bar. Alternatively, enjoy a more decadent meal in the inn's dining room, which is known for its trout dinner (reservations are recommended, and they can be made on the inn's website).

PISGAH INN

The original Pisgah Inn was built by George Weston, the former superintendent for the Biltmore Estate and a local architect. On leased land from the U.S. Forest Service, Weston broke ground in July 1919, before the Blue Ridge Parkway even existed. During construction, he and his wife camped in a tent on Pisgah Ridge for eight weeks, where Weston told a reporter, "I could live for the rest of my life."

After the Blue Ridge Parkway was built, the National Park Service became the landowner of the inn's property. Despite local outcry to salvage the original inn structures, which were showing their age and structural concerns, funding wasn't available. A more modern facility was built to house the inn north of the first site between 1963 and 1964, and the original inn was demolished in 1990; however, "the inn's doors, fireplace mantel, staircase and chestnut paneling were kept for future use," a local newspaper reported.

CONTINUED EDUCATION

Spencer, Marci. *Pisgah Inn*. Arcadia Publishing, 2020.

Spencer, Marci. *Pisgah National Forest: A History*. The History Press, 2014.

11
CATAWBA FALLS

Catawba Falls Trails map. *United States Forest Service/Uproar Concept.*

OVERVIEW

Since 2010, the public has had access to Catawba Falls thanks to the good work of the Foothills Trail Conservancy, which initially purchased the eighty-eight acres from which they spill before it transferred the deed to the U.S. Forest Service. Over the years, improvements have been made to the parking area and trail. However, none were as extensive as the work completed between 2022 and 2024, which finally granted safe and long-awaited public access to the upper falls.

Many citizens voiced their concerns during the project, fearing the work would mar the natural beauty of this special place; however, it's obvious that tremendous thought was given to the design and implementation of the hardscape in relation to the falls. Both the natural scenery and the restoration work are impressive to behold, and the area is rich with natural and human history, to boot.

THE STATS

Distance: 3.5 mile loop
Difficulty: Moderate
Elevation Gain and Loss: 833-foot gain, 833-foot loss
Maps: National Geographic no. 779 Linville Gorge, USGS 7.5' Moffitt Hill
Trailhead GPS Coordinates: 35.61335, -82.23086
Highlights: upper and lower falls, observation deck with long-range views, old hydroelectric dam and powerhouse
Notes: Bathrooms are located at the trailhead. Leashed dogs are allowed, and the trail is family friendly.
Driving Directions: From Asheville, take I-40 east to exit 73. Turn right on Catawba Falls Road before the end of the exit and follow it until it dead ends into the parking area.

HIKE DESCRIPTION

On May 31, 2024, the trail that leads to Catawba Falls, one of the most popular waterfalls in Western North Carolina, reopened after a two-year closure. In 2021, the falls were selected as a Great American Outdoors Act project for historic investment in recreation infrastructure on public lands, and work began the following year. Funding was also provided by the North Carolina State Recreational Trails Program, McDowell County, the National Forest Foundation and the G5 Trail Collective.

Upon the trail's reopening, visitors were able to safely visit the upper falls—something that wasn't possible previously. Catawba Falls held the unfortunate superlative of being McDowell County's number one trail for injuries and deaths, averaging one life-threatening injury per month for those who ignored the signs of the dangers of scrambling to the upper falls.

The hike begins on a double-wide gravel path to the right of the trailhead kiosk on the yellow-blazed River Trail. In the 1800s, the trail was used for stagecoach travel. Around 0.4 miles, you'll cross a bridge that spans the Catawba River, named for the tribe of Natives who once lived along its banks. The Cherokee word for Catawba, yi kútapu, means "people in the fork of the river."

Just before the bridge, you'll pass a defunct stone hydroelectric powerhouse. The 224-mile-long Catawba River's headwaters begin in McDowell County, near Mount Mitchell, and flow east and then south before they end in Lake Wylie on North Carolina's border with South Carolina. The river is home

Hydroelectric powerhouse ruins. *Photograph by the author.*

Lower Catawba Falls. *Photograph by the author.*

to seven North Carolina dams, the most of any river in the state, providing hydroelectric power, drinking water and flood control.

Continuing on, you'll pass the start of the new Wildflower Trail, which connects again to the River Trail in a quarter mile if you'd like to take it. If you stay on the River Trail, you'll pass an old concrete hydropower dam with three tiers of water cascading below it about 0.8 miles into the hike.

At 1.1 miles, soon after you cross another bridge, the 250-foot lower falls will come into view. This is also the start of 535 hand-built stairs that ascend a quarter mile to the base of the upper falls. Each stair was positioned by hand using a custom-built pulley system with cables anchored to the waterfall rocks. They may appear daunting, but just take your time and enjoy the waterfall views that parallel the stairs as you ascend. There are even opportunities to step off the staircase and get closer to the falls for photographs without the stairs photobombing your shot.

Eventually, you'll reach the metal observation tower. Once you reach the viewing platform, notice the scalloped railing edge whose purpose is more than decorative. It was designed with safety in mind to prevent visitors from placing objects on it that might fall off. Take a moment to soak in the long-range views out toward the Black Mountains.

Continuing upward, you'll emerge onto a dirt path with a few more steps built into the slope. Descend to the river and rock hop just downstream from the eighty-foot-tall, picture-perfect upper falls. There's just something extra special about this enchanting waterfall. Lush, evergreen foliage frames the scene of water spilling onto verdant moss-covered boulders at its base. It may not be the largest or the loudest cataract in Western North Carolina, but it takes top honors in my mind.

After soaking in the scenery, you can backtrack the way you came; however, it would be a shame to miss the Ridgeline Trail, which was also constructed during the most recent restoration period. Follow the large rock steps uphill for about half a mile before you start a long descent through the woods. Finish the loop beside the trailhead kiosk and the bathrooms.

12

CRADLE OF FORESTRY IN AMERICA

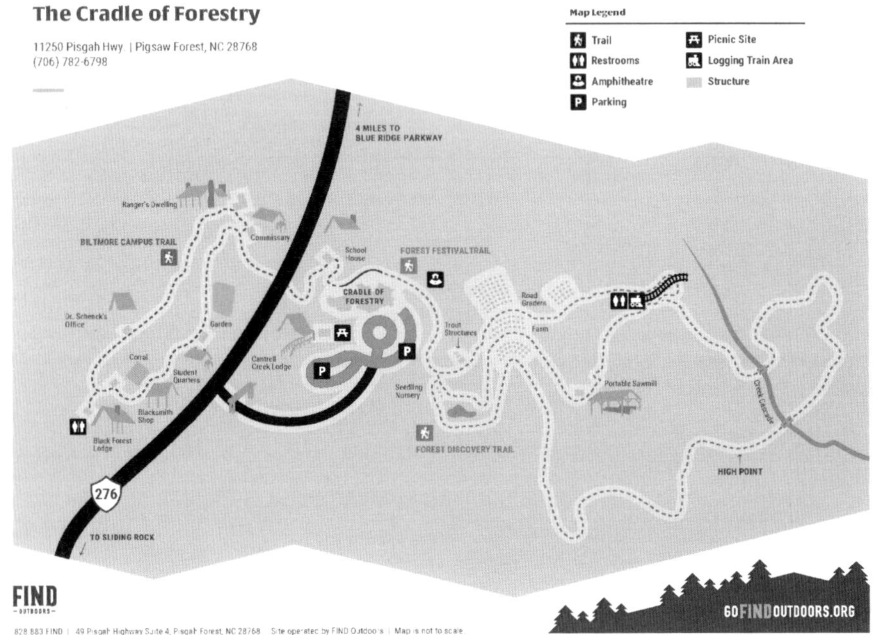

Map courtesy of FIND Outdoors, which has been in a partnership agreement with the U.S. Forest Service to manage, operate and provide educational programming at the Cradle of Forestry. *FIND Outdoors.*

OVERVIEW

History and conservation converge at the Cradle of Forestry in Pisgah National Forest, designated a National Historical Site in 1968. The 6,500-acre historic site is owned and managed by the U.S. Forest Service, but it was originally part of the 146,000 acres purchased by George Vanderbilt for his winter home, now known as the Biltmore Estate. The Cradle of Forestry's grounds and facilities pay homage to the birthplace of modern forestry in the United States, and it is also the site of the former Biltmore Forest School, the nation's first forestry school, founded in 1898 by Dr. Carl A. Schenck. The school played a pivotal role in advancing the science and practice of forestry in the late nineteenth century.

There are three interpretive trails on the property: Forest Festival, Forest Discovery and Biltmore Campus. Hiking all three trails covers less than four miles, and I highly recommend exploring each of them. Plan at least half a day for your visit, allowing ample time for you to visit the Forest Discovery Center. This engaging interpretive center offers visitors a deep dive into the history of forestry, showcasing vintage tools, forestry practices and the notable names who shaped the field. This outing is particularly well suited for families with young children. It has several hands-on exhibits for them to explore, including the popular firefighting helicopter simulator and an underground tunnel.

THE STATS

Distance: 3.9 miles (if all three trails are hiked)
Difficulty: Easy
Elevation Gain and Loss: 307-foot elevation gain, 280-foot elevation loss (if all trails are hiked)
Maps: National Geographic no. 780 Pisgah Ranger District; USGS 7.5' Shining Rock
Trailhead GPS Coordinates: 35.34973, -82.78047
Highlights: Well-preserved historical relics, family-friendly, engaging and educational indoor exhibits (Check Cradle of Forestry website for special public events.)
Notes: This space is open from mid-April to early November, and there is a nominal entrance fee for those aged sixteen and older. Restrooms are located in the Forest Discovery Center and along the interpretive trails. There are wheelchair-accessible trails. Pets are allowed on the trails and in outdoor exhibits.
Driving Directions: From the Blue Ridge Parkway, take U.S. Highway 276 South at milepost 412 for four miles until you reach the entrance on the left. From Brevard, take U.S. Highway 276 North for about fifteen miles; the entrance is located on the right.

DESCRIPTION

The well-signed trail system at the Cradle of Forestry begins behind the Forest Discovery Center building. You'll begin the hike on the Forest Festival Trail, which starts to the right. Before you reach the trail, you'll pass a large sycamore tree on the left. This tree's seed orbited the moon in 1976 on *Apollo 14* with American astronaut and former U.S. Forest Service smoke jumper Stuart Roosa. Soon after, you'll arrive at the trail and take the right fork, where you'll hike the loop in a counterclockwise direction. Shortly after it starts, the Forest Discovery Trail veers off to the right. Continue straight for now, but after you complete the loop, you should take the Forest Discovery Trail, as it is worth adding to your route (and it is included in stated mileage of this hike).

The trail is named after the annual Forest Festival, which Carl Schenck began hosting in 1908. This festival educated notable visitors about the advances in forestry and the scientific principles the school was teaching its students. The Forest Festival is still an annual fall event, with many informative and entertaining demonstrations led by forestry students and craftsmen.

The handicap-accessible trail meanders along for 1.3 miles, passing by a seedling nursery, a portable sawmill, an old homestead, an American Steam log loader and a trout hatchery. The most popular stop along the route is the Climax Engine no. 3, which was first used by Champion Fibre Company in 1914 to pull loaded logging cars along narrow-gauge railroads through forests near Robbinsville, North Carolina. The engine did not, however, spend its days only in the South. After it was retired from use in 1955, it was purchased by two Michigan railroad historians who intended to restore it. They lacked the funds to breathe new life into the engine, however, and it was purchased by the U.S. Forest Service, along with the American Steam log loader now located farther down the trail, four log cars and about four hundred feet of rails.

Once you've made your way back to the start of the Forest Festival Trail, you'll have two options. You can reduce the hiking distance by turning right and heading back to the Forest Discovery Center building, which is where the Biltmore Campus Trail begins. But I recommend veering left and getting back onto the Forest Festival Trail until the intersection on the right connects you with the Forest Discovery Trail.

For 1.3 miles, the Discovery Trail travels through a heavily wooded area, and many benches line the paved path so you can rest and soak in the sounds of the forest. It's a great trail for birding, and it's the least-used trail of the

American log loader on the Forest Festival Trail. *Photograph by the author.*

three, as it lacks the interpretive interest of the other two. If you decide to tack it on to your hike, follow it until it ends and bisects the Forest Festival Trail near the Climax Engine. At this junction, turn right and follow the remainder of the Forest Festival Trail until you arrive at the end of the loop again. This time, take a right and head back to the Forest Discovery Center, where you'll pick up the Biltmore Campus Trail.

The Biltmore Campus Trail travels through a wooded area and a short tunnel under Highway 276 before it arrives at the site of the forestry school. It passes by several of the school's structures, including Dr. Schenck's office, a commissary, student quarters and the Rock House Creek Lodge, one of fourteen Black Forest lodges built from local chestnut beams and tulip poplar siding. This lodge housed rangers who were hired by Dr. Schenck for fifty dollars a month to patrol the nearby forests and protect them from "thievery." The collective name of these lodges came about because their appearance was inspired by the architecture of structures found in the Germany's Black Forest. It's easy to imagine how the Brothers Grimm, also German, might have also been inspired by this style of architecture while writing their legendary folktales.

Biltmore Forest School students on a Climax locomotive hauling railcars loaded with logs. *Photograph taken by Carl Schenck, University of North Carolina Asheville.*

Once you've completed the Biltmore Campus loop, head back to the Forest Discovery Center building to end the hike. Before you head out, look for the Cantrell Creek Lodge near the picnic area on the front side of the Discovery Center building. It is the only other remaining Black Forest lodge, and it was moved to this location in 1979 after it was disassembled and its components flown by helicopter to this site, where it was reconstructed.

FOUNDATIONS OF FORESTRY IN THE UNITED STATES

George Vanderbilt initially had an entirely different vision for the land where the Cradle of Forestry sits. He sought the advice of Frederick Law Olmsted, who is widely regarded as the father of landscape architecture in the United States and who is famous for designing Central Park in New York City. Vanderbilt aspired to create a park with the land, but Olmsted surmised, "It's no place for a park." Instead, he encouraged the wealthy heir to focus his attention on "improving the existing woods and planting the old fields" in the wake of the destruction it had suffered from unsustainable farming practices. Gifford Pinchot, a European-trained forester, was recommended by Olmsted and hired for the job.

Pinchot proved it was possible to harvest timber for profit while maintaining a healthy forest, a model that was well established in Europe by then. Pinchot's stint with the Biltmore Estate lasted three years, and he left in 1895 after he was selected to oversee the Division of Forestry, now known as the U.S. Forest Service.

Taking Pinchot's place as the Vanderbilt forester was Dr. Carl A. Schenck, a German native. In 1898, Schenck formed the Biltmore Forest School, the first forestry school in the United States, with the original intent to train local men to assist him in the woods in the same fashion he'd

Dr. Carl Schenck in a rare moment of stillness. *Special Collections Research Center at NC State University Libraries.*

been taught. More than three hundred men graduated from the school before it closed its doors in 1913, and many of them became influential government and forestry leaders.

In a 1959 interview about his tenure as a student at the school, "Cap" Eldredge said of Schenck, "He rode two horses…nearly to death—full speed all the time. He just lectured to us three or four hours a day, and the rest of the time we were strung out behind him, traveling full speed while he tended to his duties, which he explained as he went along." Schenck's students respected him and his seemingly endless supply of energy, and some even traveled to Germany with him when school wasn't in session. Schenck had witnessed the devastation of Germany's forests and knew the importance of selectively cutting trees to foster environmental health. By 1913, Schenck's school had closed as universities began offering forestry programs, reducing the need for independent institutions. Schenck returned to Germany but left a lasting legacy in Pisgah National Forest, the first national forest east of the Mississippi, and on forest conservation in the United States.

CONTINUING EDUCATION

Schenck, Carl Alwin. *Cradle of Forestry in America: The Biltmore Forest School, 1898–1913*. Forest History Society, 1998.

13

GRANDFATHER MOUNTAIN PROFILE TRAIL

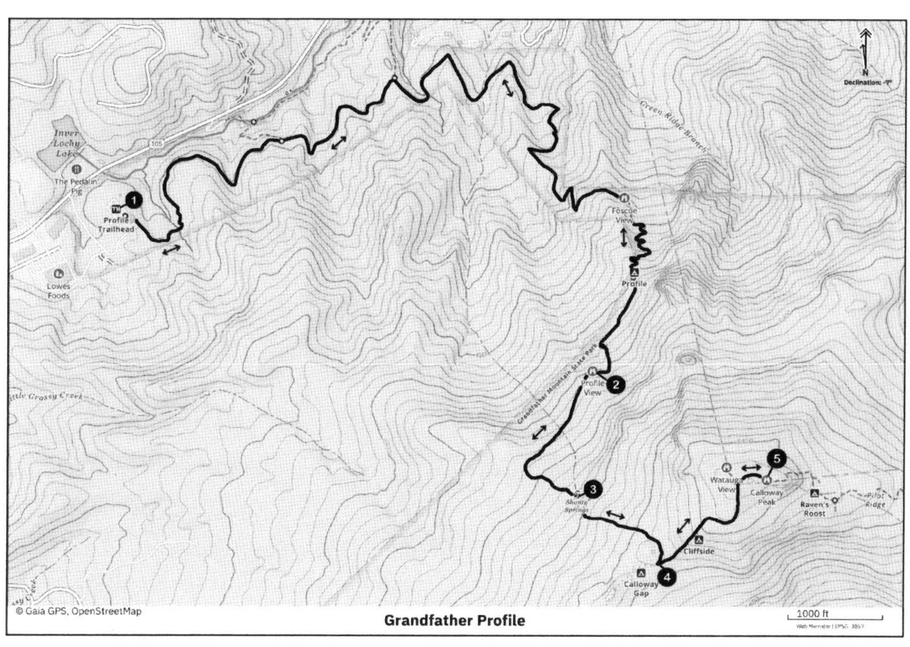

THE STATS

Distance: 7.4 miles
Difficulty: Most Difficult
Elevation Gain and Loss: 2,067-foot gain, 2,067-foot loss
Maps: National Geographic no. 779 Pisgah National Forest—Linville Gorge, Mount Mitchell; USGS 7.5' Grandfather Mountain
Trailhead GPS Coordinates: 36.11918, -81.83305
Highlights: Epic views, spruce-fir forests, wildflowers, enormous boulder gardens

Notes: Restrooms, water and picnic tables are located at the trailhead. Leashed dogs are allowed, but the nature of the terrain may be too challenging for them, with its ladders and exposed crags. There are backcountry camping options (by reservation). The trail is best hiked in late spring, summer and fall.
Driving Directions: From Asheville, take I-40 East to exit 85 for U.S. 221 North. Follow U.S. 221 North through Marion to Linville, and then turn left onto NC-105 South. After 4.3 miles, the entrance to Grandfather Mountain State Park's Profile Trail parking is on the right, 0.3 miles past the junction of Highway 184 and beyond the ABC store.

HIKE SUMMARY

When many people think of Grandfather Mountain, they recall a previous trip to Mile High Swinging Bridge, a 280-foot-long suspension bridge (which, true to its name, is 5,280 feet above sea level). It has been suspended over an 80-foot chasm since 1952. However, the privately owned portion of the mountain where the bridge still lightly swings is separate from the state park where this hike starts.

Ambitious hikers can visit the bridge without paying a fee by extending this route, but doing so adds nearly four miles to the total distance. Those four miles are some of the most technical and rugged trail miles in all of North Carolina, so I don't recommend adding them unless you're exceptionally fit (and not fearful of exposed heights).

The Grandfather Mountain Profile Trail is hardly a consolation prize. The iconic mountain treats visitors to a variety of sights along this stout but worthy hike—lush coves, enormous boulder forests, babbling creeks, spruce-fir forests and rock outcroppings where sweeping views abound. The turnaround point atop Calloway Peak (5,964 feet) is the highest mountain in the Grandfather Range, but the journey is just as rewarding as the destination.

WAYPOINTS

1. Grandfather Mountain Profile Trailhead
2. profile view (2.8 miles)
3. Shanty Spring (3.0 miles)
4. Calloway Gap (3.3 miles)
5. Calloway Peak (3.7 miles)

HIKE DESCRIPTION

This hike begins at an elevation of 4,034 feet on the back side of the restroom building adjacent to the parking area (**1**). In just over 0.1 miles on the orange-blazed trail, you'll cross a large bridge over a branch of the Watauga River. From here, the trail climbs up and down a series of timber steps and continues on a rolling course. In spring, the wildflowers are prolific here.

In 1.3 miles, you'll cross Shanty Spring Branch using well-placed, flat stepping stones. On the other side, you'll walk through the enormous boulders lining the trail. The trail continues its path upward, and at 2.2 miles, you'll arrive at Foscoe View. Elk Knob and Snake Mountain are prominent to the north, while Mount Rogers, Virginia's highest peak, is farther in the distance. The trail begins a steep climb from here until it reaches the profile campsite.

Just beyond the profile campsite, around mile 2.7, the trail traverses "Peregrine's Flight," a wet area with hundreds of artfully arranged flat boulders that pave the trail. It is a marvel, considering it was built using only hand tools, such as iron rods, shovels, pulleys and winches.

At mile 2.8, turn around to take in the profile view, the origin for this trail's name (**2**). Here, you have a bird's-eye view of the massive cliff whose jagged edge resembles the profile of an old man's face. This is one of many such views around the mountain, and some argue that it's the view that gave the mountain its name. Continuing, red spruce and fragrant Fraser fir become

Profile view of the "grandfather" of Grandfather Mountain. *Brothers Welch.*

more common. Mosses and ferns are also more common in the sun-dappled, cooler, moist air of the higher elevations.

You'll arrive at historic and picturesque Shanty Spring around mile three, which makes up the headwaters of the Watauga River that flows west toward the Mississippi River (**3**). Be sure to fill up with water if you're running low, as this is the last reliable water source until you pass it again on your descent. The path from Shanty Spring to the summit ridge is more manageable thanks to a nearly continuous path of stone steps, compliments of a construction project completed in 2021. Unlike "Peregrine's Flight," these stones were placed by machines rather than by hand.

At 3.3 miles, you'll reach Calloway Gap and turn left to follow blue-blazed Grandfather Mountain Trail to head uphill to Calloway Peak (**4**). In 0.1 miles, a side path to the right leads to Cliffside Campsite, which has sunrise views. Watauga Overlook can be reached by a short side trail located to the left in another quarter mile, where abundant evidence of civilization, including golf courses, shopping centers and hillside homes, dominates the view.

The final push to Calloway Peak's summit entails climbing several short wooden ladders to navigate over enormous rock outcrops. Calloway Peak (5,964 feet), the highest of the four summits along the Grandfather

A hiker sitting on Calloway Peak. *Sitting Bear Media.*

Mountain ridge, offers spectacular views down the spine of Grandfather Mountain's ridge and out to the Blue Ridge Parkway's Rough Ridge and Linn Cove Viaduct sections (**5**). The peaks of Linville Gorge and the Black Mountains can also be seen in the distance on a clear day.

After taking in the summit views, reverse your route and take Grandfather Mountain Trail back to Calloway Gap. Turn right at the gap to follow Grandfather Mountain Profile Trail back to the parking area.

GRANDFATHER MOUNTAIN HISTORY

The Cherokee name for this mountain is Tanawha, meaning "fabulous hawk or eagle." Later, pioneers noticed an old man's face in the mountain's cliffs and gave it an alternate moniker. Over the years, people have noticed many different faces on the mountain, but the view from Highway 105 near Boone is where the most popular of them—a reclining old, bearded man—can be seen.

In 1794, French botanist André Michaux mistakenly believed Grandfather Mountain (5,946 feet) was the tallest in North America; however, that was disproven later by Elisha Mitchell (see chapter 16). Mount Mitchell was proven to rise 738 feet higher, cresting at 6,285 feet.

Grandfather Mountain was no less impactful to early explorers, however, despite its superlative displacement. Even John Muir, founder of the Sierra Club and known for his exploration of California's Sierra Nevada, was deeply moved when he summited the massif in 1898. "I couldn't hold in, and began to jump about and sing and glory in it all," he stated in an *American Museum Journal* article.

Tourism inevitably took hold of the captivating landscape. Over time, horseback trails were replaced with roads to support automobile traffic. By 1952, Hugh McRae Morton owned the entire mountain, and he built a two-lane road to the summit so visitors could walk across his famous Mile High Swinging Bridge.

The North Carolina chapter of the Nature Conservancy came onto the scene in 1989 and began working to preserve 1,460 acres of the mountainous backcountry. In 1992, the mountain was selected to become a United Nations International Biosphere Reserve.

Morton died in 2006, and by 2008, his heirs had sold 2,600 acres of undeveloped backcountry to the State of North Carolina to create a state park. One year later, the rest of the Morton property was sold to Grandfather

Mountain Stewardship Foundation, "a nonprofit organization that continues to make the property accessible to the public, devoting all resources to preservation, conservation, education and recreation," according to the foundation's website.

CONTINUING EDUCATION

Johnson, Randy. *Grandfather Mountain: A History and Guide to an Appalachian Icon*. University of North Carolina Press, 2016.

14

SHELTON LAUREL

HICKEY FORK TO CAMP CREEK BALD

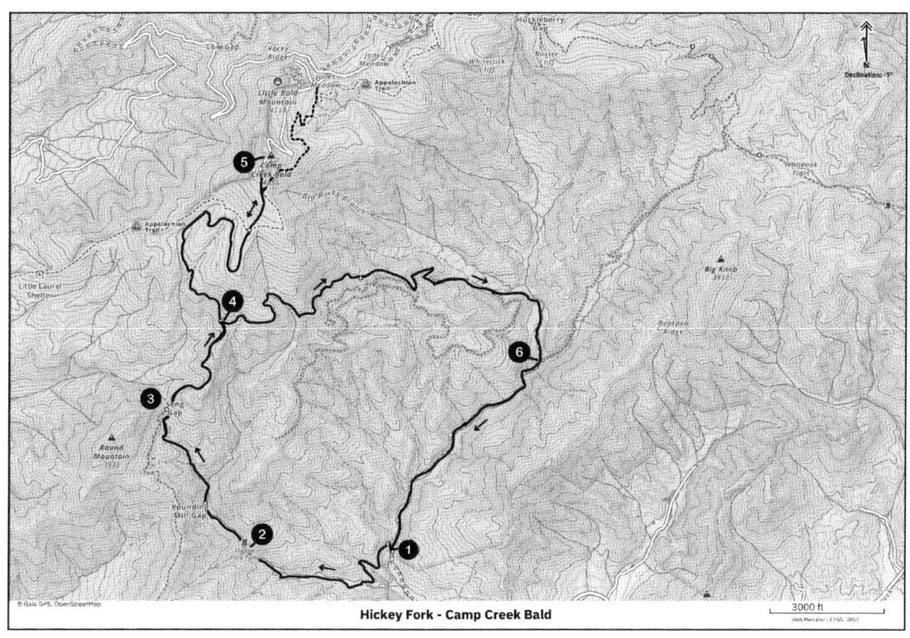

Hickey Fork - Camp Creek Bald

OVERVIEW

If challenging hikes that offer a little of everything, minus the crowds, appeal to you, prioritize this route. Located in the remote Shelton Laurel Backcountry, this route rises high above the Hickey Fork Watershed, passing cascades and a waterfall before reaching a lookout tower with unconventional design. If superlatives were awarded to the state's remaining lookout towers, this one would surely be nominated for 'Most Likely to Be Mistaken for a Spaceship.

On a clear day, you'll spot iconic peaks in the far distance at Camp Creek Bald's summit. A high-end neighborhood and ski run were both planned to take advantage of these same views, but the project failed for various reasons during the 1970s and 1980s. But the nearby Shelton Laurel community has a much more tragic story tethered to it, dating all the way back to the Civil War.

If the hike's remote nature or length doesn't appeal to you, an easier route to the lookout tower is described at the end of this chapter.

THE STATS

Distance: 10.8 miles
Difficulty: Most Difficult
Elevation Gain and Loss: 2,705-foot gain, 2,692-foot loss
Maps: USGS 7.5' White Rock, Greystone; National Geographic no. 782 French Broad and Nolichucky Rivers
Trailhead GPS: 35.99448, -82.70470 (the Jones Meadow trailhead coordinates are 36.02972, -82.70983)
Highlights: Lookout tower, waterfall, panoramic views, solitude
Notes: Leashed dogs are allowed. This is a remote trailhead with limited parking. The graves of those killed in the Shelton Laurel Massacre are located on private property.
Driving Directions: From Asheville, take I-26W to exit 19A to get on U.S.-25 North/U.S.-70 West toward Marshall. In 21 miles, continue straight onto NC-208 North. After 3.4 miles, turn right onto NC-212 North. Drive for 7 miles and then turn left onto Hickey Fork Road. The parking area and trailhead are about 1 mile down this road.

If you are hiking the shorter alternate route to the lookout tower from Jones Meadow, follow the previous directions until the intersection of NC-208 and NC-212 North. Instead of taking a right on NC-212 North, turn left to continue NC-208 for 6 more miles. You'll then cross into Tennessee where the road changes to TN-70. Turn right on Viking Mountain Road and follow it for 8.2 miles until you reach a parking pullout on the southwest end of Jones Meadow.

WAYPOINTS

1. Hickey Fork Trailhead
2. Hickey Fork Falls (1.1 miles)
3. Seng Gap (2.3 miles)
4. Camp Creek Bald (4.8 miles)
5. White Oak Flats Trail junction (6.8 miles)

HIKE DESCRIPTION

Hickey Fork Trail starts 120 feet north of the trailhead, past a metal gate on the left side of Forest Road 465 (**1**). Descend the stone steps and cross East Prong Hickey Fork on a curved log bridge. The trail bears right and passes through a rhododendron tunnel, paralleling the creek before it turns away from it to the left at 0.1 miles.

Rhododendrons are ubiquitous for the next couple of miles, climbing the hillsides and covering the creek banks. At 0.5 miles, descend a couple of stone steps and rock hop West Prong Hickey Fork; then you will encounter a tributary crossing on an old log bridge. At mile 1, the trail ascends in earnest. It's a manageable grade initially; however, pace yourself, because you have a long (and steeper) climb ahead. The West Prong Hickey Fork parallels the trail, rushing down a long rockslide into an unseen ravine.

At 1.1 miles, the 25-foot-tall Hickey Fork Falls come into view on the right (**2**). Without recent rain, the falls may not be overly impressive, but their remote location (and the fact that you'll probably have them to yourself) makes up for it.

At 1.7 miles, the trail pulls away from West Prong Hickey Fork, and the grade steepens significantly, climbing 400 feet in the next 0.3 miles. At 2.3 miles, you'll arrive at Seng Gap (**3**). Turn right and continue your ascent on the yellow-blazed Hickey Fork Trail (which was formerly called Pounding Mill Trail, and trail signage may still reflect the old name).

Just under three miles, you'll arrive at another signed junction and continue to the left, still following Hickey Fork Trail. In another half mile, the trail levels out, some amid a vibrant beech grove. Just above you, to the left and along the ridgeline, is the Appalachian Trail (AT).

At mile 4.5, you'll cross over the AT, earning bragging rights for hiking its entire *width*. In another 0.2 miles, a wooden sign points out the direction you need to follow to reach Camp Creek Bald, which is where you're headed.

This blue-blazed trail continues steeply for 0.2 miles. You'll emerge into a clearing with several communication towers and structures. Follow the faint trail to the right of the chain-link fence surrounding the orange-topped tower, or climb the road to the left. Either way, you'll arrive at Camp Creek Bald Lookout Tower, which straddles the North Carolina–Tennessee border and was built in 1928 (**4**).

Originally, the twenty-one-foot-tall steel tower had a more traditional, square live-in cab, but it was replaced in the 1960s with the current circular cab that is reminiscent of a flying saucer. Earl Shaffer, the first person to thru hike the AT, stayed in the original cab on April 25, 1948, on his long journey to Maine, and he was kept company by Ed Tweed, the watchman at the time. Both men were probably grateful for companionship in this remote area. In 1968, the AT was rerouted to bypass the summit and avoid private property that was slated for development.

The cab isn't open to the public, but a flight of steps leads to a landing to take in most of the view. The Black Mountains, including Mount Mitchell, are visible to the southeast, nearly thirty-one miles away. The grassy bald to the east is Big Bald, and Mount Pisgah's recognizable summit looms far to the south.

Camp Creek Bald Lookout. *Photograph by the author.*

As the crow flies, about a mile from the summit of Camp Creek Bald, in the valley below (on private property), rests a plaque with thirteen names inscribed. Nearby, scattered headstones, some unmarked, dot the forest floor. The plaque was placed by the Shelton family in the 1960s, and the names on the headstones are those of men and boys, all between the ages of thirteen and sixty, who died in January 1863 in the Shelton Laurel Massacre.

Also, about six miles farther north, along the Appalachian Trail, is another cluster of graves related to the Civil War. Buried there are Millard Haire, William Shelton and David Shelton, all from Madison County and all Union soldiers. They were ambushed and killed by Confederate soldiers as they returned home for a family gathering. It's understandable why Madison County carries the sobering moniker "Bloody Madison."

Retrace your steps back to the junction with White Oak Flats Trail at 6.8 miles (**5**) and take a left onto it. The trail climbs and then levels before dropping sharply to the right at mile 7.2. Cross a boulder field over the fledgling West Prong Hickey Fork at 8.3 miles; then turn left and head downhill into Big Rocky Branch valley instead of taking the old logging road on the right. In winter, the Baxter Cliffs are visible on the mountainside at eye level.

Continue downhill, where you'll emerge onto FR 465 around the 9-mile mark. FR 465 dead ends just to the left of this junction, and there's a gated forest service road to the right and up a hill, but you'll keep going straight. East Prong Hickey Fork parallels the road, offering good company until you reach the trailhead and your waiting car, 1.8 miles ahead.

SHELTON LAUREL MASSACRE

During the Civil War, Colonel Lawrence M. Allen, the leader of the Sixty-Fourth Confederate Regiment, was one of the few people in Madison County who enslaved his laborers. Many nearby farming residents and those in the impoverished Shelton Laurel community couldn't relate to the Confederate agenda of slavery and secession, and some kept their allegiance to the Union. When the Confederacy passed conscription laws in 1862, men in the community were forced to enlist. They often defected quickly and returned home to provide for their struggling families.

Under orders from Governor Zebulon Vance, Confederate soldiers in Marshall withheld salt from these "disloyal" mountain families of Shelton

Laurel. Salt had already been rationed due to the Union's blockade of its delivery from Europe, and it was one of the most valuable commodities of the day. It played a critical role in surviving the long, harsh mountain winters, since it was used for curing and preserving meat.

One bitterly cold January day, some of the men from Shelton Laurel rode into Marshall demanding their salt ration after the women of the community had been denied it. When their pleas were also rejected, they didn't back down and began looting community buildings and homes, including the home of Colonel Lawrence Allen. Allen's wife and children, who were sick with scarlet fever, were inside the home at the time.

Allen and Lieutenant Colonel James Keith, second in command to Allen and his cousin, were enraged when they received word of what had happened. They and their troops headed to the Shelton Laurel community, where they proceeded to threaten the women of the community so they'd reveal the whereabouts of the looters. According to the late Civil War expert Phillip Shaw Paludan in this book *Victims*, the Confederate soldiers tied one woman to a tree and put her infant in the snow at her feet in the hopes she would cave. The women, however, bravely kept their silence.

Allen and Keith rounded up fifteen men, only five of whom were believed to have been part of the looting. They held them captive in a local resident's home, but two prisoners were able to escape that night. The following morning, the Confederates marched the remaining thirteen men for several miles before they executed them in groups of five, five and three. Some of the soldiers who fired the fatal shots were hesitant, likely because three of the boys they were killing were only thirteen, fourteen and fifteen years old. They were told by those in command to either shoot the looters or take their place. The bodies were placed in a shallow grave, where hogs ravaged the corpses that evening.

> *I think the single most disturbing aspect of the Shelton Laurel Massacre was the youngest victim was also the last one to die.*
>
> —*Ron Rash (author of* The World Made Straight, *which draws heavily from this event)*

The following day, a woman known to locals as Granny Judy, who was an aunt to two of those killed, along with her children, gathered the remains onto an ox sled and carried them to their current and final resting place.

JONES MEADOW HISTORY AND AN ALTERNATE ROUTE TO CAMP CREEK BALD LOOKOUT TOWER

This alternative two-mile loop route, indicated by the dashed line on the map at the beginning of this chapter, starts at Jones Meadow, which was used as an emergency landing strip during World War II. Until 1968, it was also part of the Appalachian Trail. The most notable history that surrounds Jones Meadow, however, is a failed business venture that was started in the 1960s.

A developer purchased Jones Meadow and the ridgeline below it with visions of building a ski resort. Viking Mountain Resort eventually had two ski runs along with Valhalla Inn, a posh lodge and restaurant. Guest cabins, referred to as "roundettes," were also built in the same shape as the nearby lookout tower, perhaps not so coincidentally. The resort failed in 1972 after one season, due to financial difficulties and the challenges of keeping snow on the slopes.

To hike to the tower from the Jones Meadow pullout parking area, follow Camp Creek Bald Road in a southwest direction for about 500 feet until you see a blue-blazed side trail on the left that leads downhill. Follow the side trail for 0.1 miles and turn right on the white-blazed Appalachian Trail. At the 1-mile mark, you'll arrive at a four-way intersection, with Hickey Fork Trail on the left. Turn right and follow the spur trail to the lookout tower.

You can either retrace your steps or make a loop by walking gravel Camp Creek Bald Road near the tower back to Jones Meadow.

CONTINUING EDUCATION

Rash, Ron. *The World Made Straight.* Picador, 2007.

15

LAUREL RIVER TRAIL

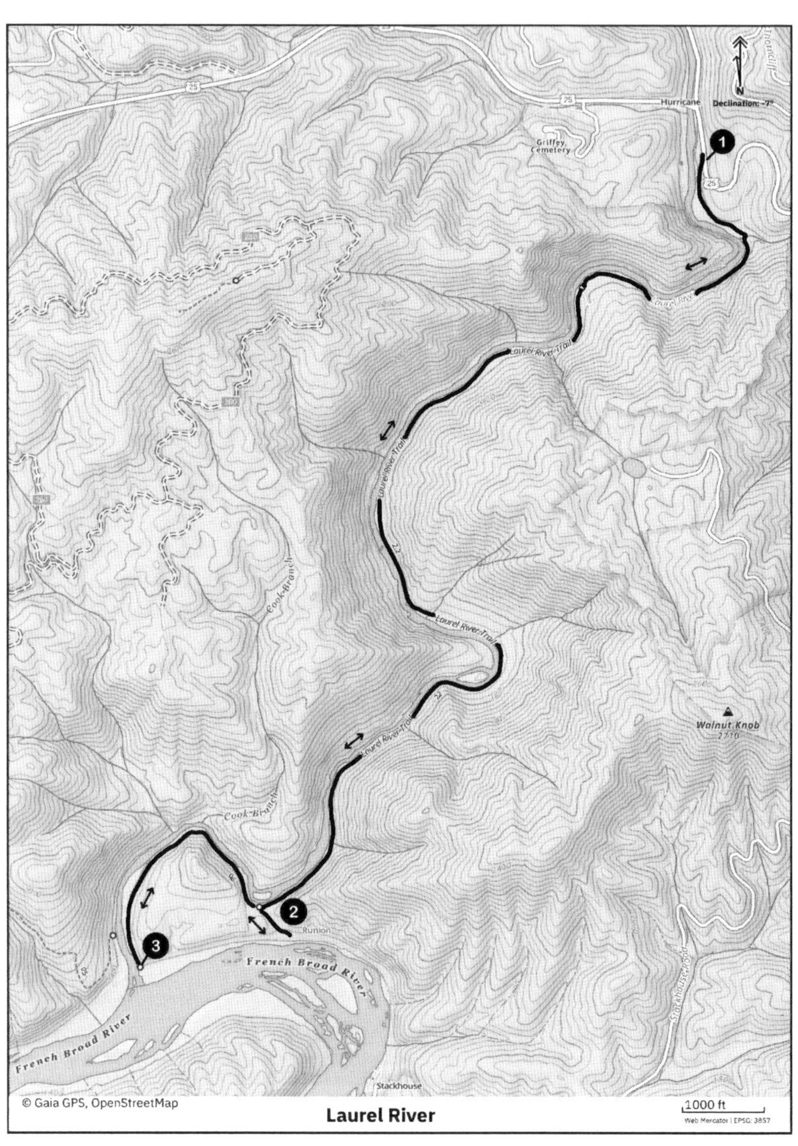

OVERVIEW

I lived in Western North Carolina for twenty-five years before I set foot on the Laurel River Trail. Don't make the same mistake I did; prioritize this rails-to-trail path sooner, because it's a treasure in every season. In spring, wildflowers are prolific; in the heat of summer, the cool waters of Big Laurel Creek invite you to explore an abundance of swimming holes; during fall, the steep walls of Laurel Creek Gorge are awash in autumnal colors; and even in winter, since the trail never crests two thousand feet, it's a viable option compared to higher-elevation hikes. It's also one of the flattest trails in the region, making it a great choice for families.

Laurel River Trail follows the path of an old railroad bed that was once used to carry logs to a sawmill in the early 1900s. Near the turnaround point for this out-and-back hike, you'll discover the ghost town of Runion, which was a thriving community with about 1,200 residents at its peak. In addition to the sawmill, which anchored the town, Runion had a school, a church and even its own baseball team, which played against nearby lumber company teams on an island in the French Broad River, the only unoccupied level land.

THE STATS

Distance: 7.2 miles, out and back
Difficulty: Moderate (due to distance, but it's one of the flattest trails in the region)
Elevation Gain and Loss: 220-foot gain, 220-foot loss
Maps: National Geographic no. 782 French Broad and Nolichucky Rivers, Cherokee and Pisgah National Forests; USGS Hot Springs
Trailhead GPS Coordinates: 35.91248, -82.75671
Highlights: Creekside walk, wildflowers, year-round accessibility, kid friendly, historic logging community ruins, French Broad River views
Notes: Leashed dogs are allowed. The first 0.7 miles of the trail pass through a private right-of-way. The trail can get muddy with rain.
Driving Directions: From Exit 19 on Interstate 26, follow U.S. 25/70 north toward Marshall for about twenty miles. The large gravel parking area for the trailhead is located on the left, near the intersection of NC-208 and U.S. 25/70.

WAYPOINTS

1. Laurel River Trailhead
2. Runion ruins (3.0 miles)
3. confluence of the French Broad and Laurel Rivers (3.6 miles)

HIKE DESCRIPTION

From the parking area and trailhead, head south on the wide trail, which parallels U.S. 25/70 for a short distance (**1**). After passing a gate on the left, the trail descends to the old logging grade. In just under a quarter mile, you'll pass a small cottage on the left and continue following the trail, which parallels a wide right turn in Big Laurel Creek. You'll then pass under a high bluff whose lower section was blasted away to create the railway. Until you've hiked 0.7 miles, resist the urge to venture to the creek since you're passing through a right-of-way on private property.

The trail narrows into a single track upon entering national forest property. At the one-mile mark, you'll walk around a large boulder in the middle of the trail. From here on, Big Laurel Creek invites you to enjoy its banks, rocks and pools.

In 1.6 miles, you'll notice the stone wall along the stream, which was built to support the railroad above it. There's a particularly deep pool in this area of the creek. Shortly after, a couple of larger rapids appear just before a flat area beside the trail with a campsite. An island also emerges in the creek, and its length extends for the next 0.4 miles.

Just under two and a half miles into the hike, the creek travels through the most narrow and rugged part of the gorge, barreling through a stone-lined channel. The gorge soon widens again before it reaches the former site of Runion at the three-mile point. You'll know you're there when you notice concrete walls alongside the trail.

Scattered ruins, including crumbling chimneys, machinery parts, and a concrete base of a flagpole with hand-carved inscriptions of "Freedom," "Forever" and "October 1, 1917" are tucked away in the woods and can be found if you're willing to poke around a bit. There were once simple four-room houses here, built for mill workers and their families, that were rented out for three dollars a month. They were not built to stand the test of time, however, so you won't find any of them now.

A quiet pool on Big Laurel Creek. *Misty Gilbert.*

Runion ruins. *Misty Gilbert.*

Jan C. Plemmons, the author of *A Visit to Runion: A Ghost Town of Western North Carolina*, sheds a light on how the town was named: "There was supposedly a mailman that walked and delivered mail from Stackhouse down to Putnam. He had a lame foot, and they called him 'Paddlefoot.' His last name was Runion. So they named the town after the mailman."

Advertisements in the *Asheville Citizen Times* alerted locals to various jobs in Runion. There was no ambiguity about who would be an appropriate candidate for employment in one such advertisement from 1913: "Wanted—lumber pilers, yard men, mill hands, teamsters and section hands. Wages from $1.50 to $2.50 per day. Pay every two weeks. No boys wanted. Only sober, steady men need apply."

In 1916, a flood severely damaged the Laurel River Logging Company's mill in Runion and the railroad tracks leading from it, and this started the community's downward spiral. Compounding the flood damages, World War I required much of the mill's workforce in 1918. Those who remained began moving to more populated cities like Asheville to restart their lives.

It may be a bit overgrown in the summer, but look for the spur trail to the left, which leads past some of the remaining artifacts and what was once the heart of Runion (**2**). The path dead ends at the active Norfolk Southern rail line. At the junction with the spur trail, the Laurel River Trail continues for another 0.6 miles before it ends at the confluence of Big Laurel Creek and the mighty French Broad River, which the Norfolk Southern rail line crosses over on a trellis (**3**).

Big Laurel Creek contributes to the over four thousand miles of streams and rivers feeding the French Broad River, which is estimated to be between 260 and 325 million years old, one of the oldest rivers in the world. The Cherokee gave the river its first names: Tahkeeostee, or "racing waters," and Agiqua, or "long man." But European settlers coined it the French Broad River to distinguish it from North Carolina's other Broad River.

In Western North Carolina, plenty of recreation opportunities exist on the 218-mile-long French Broad River as it flows through Transylvania, Henderson, Buncombe and Madison Counties. These activities range from adrenaline-fueled whitewater rafting trips to lazy floats on inner tubes. Starting at its headwaters west of Rosman, North Carolina, and ending at the Holston River in Knoxville, Tennessee, the French Broad River is one of the few rivers that flows north instead of south. Only when the French Broad terminates at the Holston River does its water head south, where it travels all the way to the Gulf of Mexico via the paths of the Holston, Tennessee, Ohio and Mississippi Rivers.

To complete the hike, return to the main trail and follow it back to the trailhead, about three and a half miles away.

CONTINUING EDUCATION

Plemmons, Jan C. *A Visit to Runion: A Ghost Town of Western North Carolina.* Self-published, 2022.

16

MOUNT MITCHELL LOOP

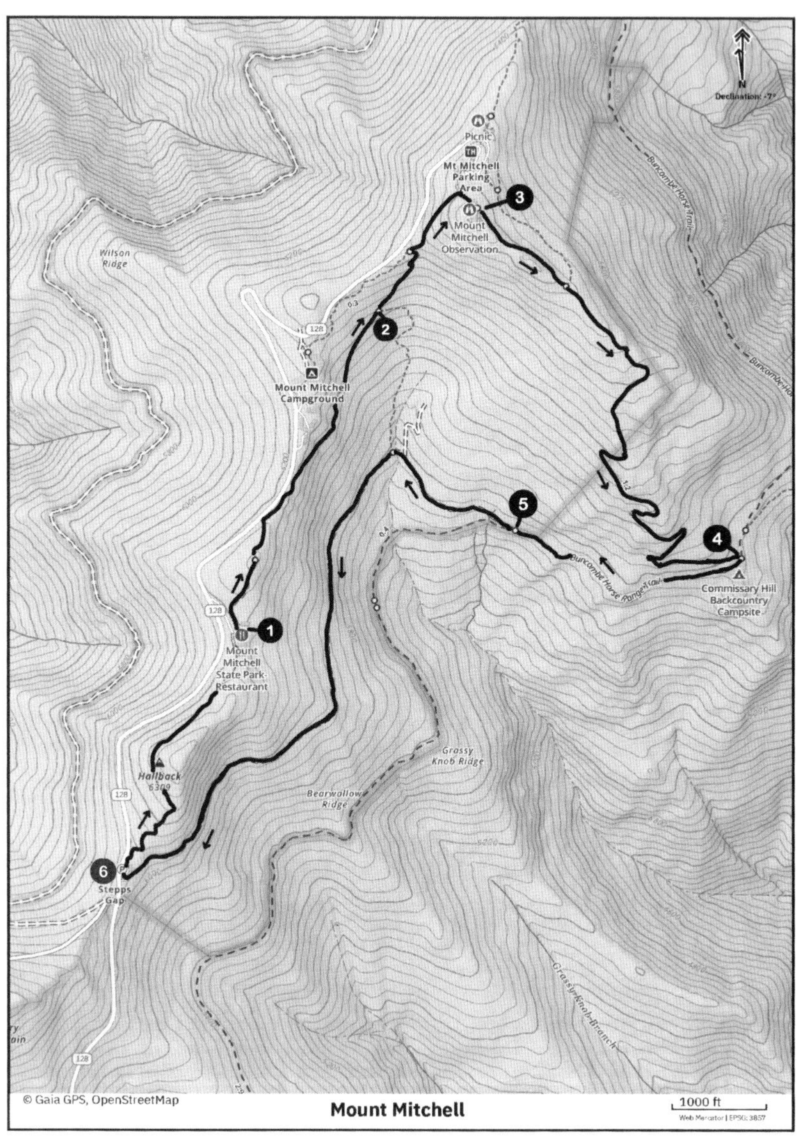

OVERVIEW

Standing tall at a height of 6,684 feet, Mount Mitchell (known as Attakulla in Cherokee) not only reaches higher than any other peak in North Carolina, but it also boasts the title of being the tallest mountain east of the Mississippi River. The mountain is seated in the highest-elevation state park of North Carolina that bears the same name, and its visitors glimpse what it would be like to hike over 2,000 miles farther north, as far as the Canadian wilderness, since every 1,000 feet gained in elevation equals a climate change of about 300 miles to the north.

This loop hike leads you through ancient spruce-fir forests before summiting Mount Mitchell. Then, it descends to an old railroad line that once brought visitors to the mountain. Big views abound, and even the trailhead at Stepps Gap is special since the newly renovated Mount Mitchell Restaurant sits nearby. This is a fun family hike, and a promised post-hike meal at the restaurant is often an appealing "carrot" for both young and old.

THE STATS

Distance: 5.5 miles
Difficulty: Moderate
Elevation Gain and Loss: 1,017-foot gain, 1,082-foot loss
Maps: USGS 7.5' Mount Mitchell, NC; Mount Mitchell State Park
Trailhead GPS Coordinates: 35.75299, -82.27379
Highlights: Highest point in North Carolina and east of the Mississippi River, panoramic views, high-elevation forest
Notes: Mount Mitchell State Park is open year-round, but check for Blue Ridge Parkway closures, especially in winter. Restrooms are located at the state park visitor center, restaurant, gift shop and snack bar. Leashed dogs are allowed on the trails.
Driving Directions: From Asheville, take the Blue Ridge Parkway north for thirty-four miles to milepost 355. Turn left on NC-128 into Mount Mitchell State Park and follow this road three miles to the restaurant's parking area on the right.

WAYPOINTS

1. Old Mitchell Trailhead
2. Camp Alice Trail junction (0.8 miles)
3. Mount Mitchell summit and observation deck (1.4 miles)
4. Commissary Trail/Buncombe Horse Trail intersection (2.9 miles)
5. Buncombe Horse Trail veers left (3.5 miles)
6. Stepps Gap (4.9 miles)

HIKE DESCRIPTION

To start the hike, look for the single-track path of the yellow-blazed Old Mitchell Trail north of the restaurant (**1**). The trail ducks into the woods and begins to climb gently, initially running parallel to NC-128.

Just after 0.4 miles, the trail crosses through a power line clearing. From here, the tread becomes more technical as the rugged path winds its way through boulder-strewn sections with slabs of earth made slick and muddy by nearby seeps. Steps and bridges will help you through this section, but it's still slow going.

At 0.8 miles, the trail intersects with Camp Alice Trail, which veers right and heads downhill to a point you'll reach later, but stay to the left to continue down the Old Mitchell Trail (**2**). At the 1-mile mark, the Campground Spur Trail feeds in from the left; continue straight until the trail dead ends onto the paved summit trail. Turn right onto this path; you'll pass by the environmental education center on your left and the Balsam Nature Trail before you spiral up to the summit observation platform.

At the base of the platform is Elisha Mitchell's grave, which reminds visitors of the storied history of the mountain (see *Mountains of Controversy* at the end of this chapter). The current observation platform is the fifth to be erected on the summit. The first was built in 1916, but a sturdier stone tower replaced it in 1926. Due to safety concerns, it was dismantled in 1959. In 1960, an architect-designed tower emerged, only to be removed in 2006. The current platform, which complies with ADA standards, now sits where the tower once stood. The platform holds signage that indicates the four cardinal directions and distant points on the horizon; however, statistically speaking, you have only a 50 percent chance of seeing the peaks the signs reference, since the summit is enveloped in clouds or fog half the time (**3**).

Elisha Mitchell's grave in front of the summit observation platform. *Photograph by the author.*

After you leave the observation platform, turn right onto the Balsam Nature Trail and walk past a few interpretive signs. At the 1.7-mile mark, join the Mount Mitchell Trail by staying straight, and head downhill for the next 1.25 miles. In just under 3 miles, turn right onto the Buncombe Horse Trail/Commissary Trail (**4**).

At 3.5 miles, the Buncombe Horse Trail veers left, but stay to the right to continue following the Commissary Trail (**5**), which follows an old logging railroad line that eventually morphed into a tourist rail line. That line ran until 1919, when it was turned into a toll road for motorists who were visiting the mountain. The road served this purpose from 1922 to 1939, when the Blue Ridge Parkway was opened. At mile 3.8, Camp Alice Trail, whose northern end you'll have encountered earlier, enters on the right. The camp was the destination for those who were visiting the mountain via the rail line. A dining hall and platform tents awaited visitors.

Continue your gentle ascent until you reach Stepps Gap (**6**) and the state park office just under five miles into your hike. Walk around the building (which has restrooms) and look for the Old Mitchell Trail. Follow this trail for half a mile, contouring the western slope of Mount Hallback, and you'll end your hike as the trail emerges from the woods and onto the grounds of the park's restaurant, where you can enjoy a well-deserved post-hike meal.

MOUNTAINS OF CONTROVERSY

Considerable controversy and competition surrounded Mount Mitchell's summit long before there was a path leading to it. The mountain, once called Black Dome, is named for Dr. Elisha Mitchell, a nineteenth-century professor and geologist at the University of North Carolina–Chapel Hill. It was thought that nearby Grandfather Mountain was the tallest mountain in all North America after French botanist André Michaux wrote in his journal in 1794, "Reached the summit of the highest mountain in all of North America."

Mitchell took a trip to Grandfather Mountain in 1838 to record elevation data, and this piqued his initial curiosity about the Black Mountains' heights in the distance. On that trip, it is believed he spent his first night sleeping in the woods. He fretted and tossed under the rock ledge where he and his companions camped, looking at his timepiece "a good many times to see if it was not nearly morning."

Fueled by his curiosity on Grandfather Mountain and aided by two local men who intimately knew the rugged terrain of the Black Mountains and served as his guides, Mitchell visited the range for three summers over a span of two decades to determine which of its peaks was indeed the tallest in the state.

He made it known to his backcountry companions that he didn't fancy spending the night in the woods ever again, despite the extra effort this would require of him physically each day. Unfortunately, his reluctance to sleep outdoors left him little time on the range's summits to record visual references to substantiate his elevation research. In those days, ample time was critical to record barometric pressures and take comprehensive notes about the topography and landscape, which were used to accurately substantiate claims.

In 1855, one of Mitchell's former students, U.S. senator and amateur geologist Thomas Clingman, disputed Mitchell's findings that he'd summited the highest peak after reading his vague accounts. Spurred by his skepticism of Mitchell's account and his ego to be the first to summit the state's highest peak, Clingman made a trip to the suspected highest summit. The men were not in disagreement about which peak was the tallest but rather which of them had summited it first: Mitchell in 1844 or Clingman in 1855.

Once friends, the men became bitter rivals. For two years, they debated their positions in the press, and the story took as many twists and turns as the modern trails on the mountain, as is thoroughly detailed in Timothy Silver's

Mount Mitchell and the Black Mountains: An Environmental History of the Highest Peaks in Eastern America.

The feud ultimately cost Mitchell his life. In June 1857, he returned to the Black Mountains to set the record straight by taking new measurements from the peak he believed he had submitted previously. Tragically, he fell during his solo expedition and died in an isolated ravine at the base of what is now named Mitchell Falls. His body was found and recovered by searchers eleven days later. They discovered his broken timepiece still on his body, its hands arrested at 8:19:56 p.m., presumably the time, to the second, of his fatal fall.

In the wake of Mitchell's death and through savvy campaigning by his advocates, public opinion was swayed in favor of Mitchell summiting the peak first. In 1882, the peak formerly known as Black Dome was officially named Mount Mitchell by the United States Geological Survey, and Mitchell's body was brought to its final resting place on the summit in 1858, after having first been interred in Asheville.

To this day, however, scholars debate whose story is the correct one. Interestingly, modern calculations have determined that Mitchell's measurement of one of the peaks in 1835 was only 12 feet lower than Mount

Visitors at Elisha Mitchell Memoriam, circa 1920s. *Courtesy of the State Archives of North Carolina.*

Mitchell's actual height of 6,684 feet. This added yet another plot twist and left experts wondering if Mitchell had, in fact, summited his namesake mountain during his first trip to the Black Mountains in 1835, even though he wasn't convinced he had done so until 1844. Nearby Clingmans Peak, which is the peak Clingman claimed Mitchell had mistakenly thought was the highest, was eventually named for Thomas Clingman.

After Mitchell's death, Clingman turned his attention to measuring the Smokies' peaks, suspecting some of them might be even taller than the mountain he and Mitchell had fought over. In 1859, Clingmans Dome (6,643 feet tall) was named in his honor; however, in 2022, members of the Eastern Band of Cherokee began advocating for Clingmans Dome's name to be reverted to Kuwohi, the original name given to the mountain by Cherokee, which means "mulberry place." On September 18, 2024, the U.S. Board of Geographic Names voted in favor of the formal request by the Eastern Band of the Cherokee Indians to change the name of Clingmans Dome to Kuwohi.

CONTINUING EDUCATION

Bennett, Jonathan Howard, and Divid Biddix. *Mount Mitchell.* Images of America. Arcadia Publishing, 2015.

Silver, Timothy. *Mount Mitchell and the Black Mountains: An Environmental History of the Highest Peaks in Eastern America*. University of North Carolina Press, 2003.

17

MOUNTAINS TO SEA TRAIL

PLOTT BALSAM RANGE

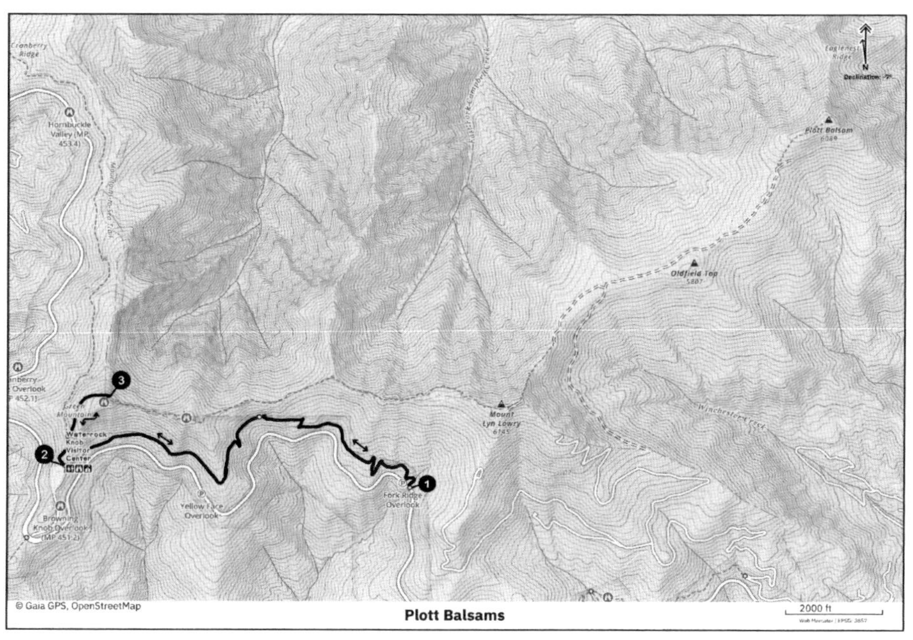

Plott Balsams

OVERVIEW

The Plott Balsam Range stretches over 142 square miles from the Tuckaseegee River valley in Jackson County to Maggie Valley in Haywood County. Many of the Blue Ridge Parkway's visitors hike a short but stout trail to the summit of Waterrock Knob, the range's highest peak, where they are rewarded with panoramic views of the surrounding mountains.

This route to the 6,292-foot-tall summit, however, provides more solitude and scenery because it starts on the Mountains to Sea Trail. The Plott

Balsams have stories to tell, some of them a stark reminder of life's fragility; however, as you gaze at the ridgeline of the distant peaks from Waterrock Knob, it's hard not to be inspired by the rugged beauty of this range.

The Plott Balsams are named for the Plott family and their namesake Plott hound, which became the North Carolina state dog by legislative decree on August 12, 1989. The Plott hound is one of only four breeds that was started in the United States, and it is the only dog breed officially recognized to have originated in North Carolina. Johannes Plott, a German immigrant gamekeeper, brought ancestors of the breed with him to Carrabus County in 1750.

THE STATS

Distance: 5.4 miles
Difficulty: Moderate
Elevation Gain and Loss: 1,130-foot gain, 1,130-foot loss
Maps: National Geographic no. 785 Nantahala and Cullasaja Gorges—Nantahala National Forest; USGS 7.5' Sylva North, Hazelwood
Trailhead GPS Coordinates: 35.45944, -83.11723
Highlights: Panoramic views, diverse flora and fauna, Waterrock Knob Visitor Center
Notes: Leashed dogs are allowed. Seasonal bathrooms are available at the Waterrock Knob parking area. Check the Blue Ridge Parkway's website for real-time road closure information. Mount Lyn Lowry is easily visible from the Lyn Lowry Overlook at mile marker 445.2.
Driving Directions: From Waynesville, take U.S. 74 to the Blue Ridge Parkway junction at Balsam Gap and head south on the parkway. After 5.4 miles, turn left into the Fork Ridge Overlook parking area at mile marker 449. The trail begins on the opposite side of the parkway.

WAYPOINTS

1. Mountains to Sea Trailhead
2. Waterrock Knob Trail junction (2.2 miles)
3. Waterrock Knob summit (2.7 miles)

HIKE DESCRIPTION

Cross over the Blue Ridge Parkway from the Fork Ridge Overlook and look for the Mountains to Sea Trail (MST), which heads into the woods up a short flight of wooden steps. **(1)** On your left, you'll pass a fence with views of Fork Ridge Overlook. Continue the rolling ascent along the southern flanks of Mount Lyn Lowry, Browning Knob and Waterrock Knob, which rise high above you.

In the midsummer, brambles line the trail in short, exposed sections, providing a sweet snack of blackberries. Nearly 2 miles in, an enormous spruce greets you on the left, and at 2.2 miles, the dirt path you've been walking bisects the paved path that leads left to the Waterrock Knob parking area and visitor center and right to Waterrock's summit **(2)**.

If you'd like, head downhill to the seasonal visitor center (and bathrooms) before continuing. It's a great place to learn more about the natural and cultural history of the area.

If you opt to skip the visitor center, turn right and continue the uphill climb. You'll pass through a stone overlook with a view of Yellow Face to the southwest. At 2.3 miles, the MST veers off to the left to continue toward its western terminus at Kuwohi (formerly Clingmans Dome) in Great Smoky Mountains National Park, but you'll continue climbing the paved path to the summit of Waterrock Knob at mile 2.7 **(3)**.

After taking in the summit views, return the way you ascended, but make sure to stop and look to the east (right), just below the summit. You'll catch a glimpse of some of the peaks whose flanks you traversed earlier on the hike.

The peak in the near distance is Browning Knob, which has a tragic claim to fame. On November 24, 1983 (Thanksgiving Day), a Cessna 414A with two passengers was en route from West Chicago, Illinois, and only 11 miles from Sylva, North Carolina, its destination, when it crashed into the mountain, killing both passengers. The pilot was impaired with a blood alcohol level of .04 percent, and the flying conditions that night were less than favorable, with rain and fog. The last radio contact was made about 1 mile from the crash site when the plane was at 6,100 feet, 140 feet below Browning Knob's summit.

The engines were removed from the site, but the fuselage, wings and associated debris were left behind. Over the years, the wreckage became increasingly popular to visit. The National Park Service had reservations, for fear that hikers would get lost or injured while trying to find the wreckage, which wasn't on a designated trail. They also had concerns that visitors would

Waterrock Knob (*left*) and Jones Knob (*center*, renamed Mount Lyn Lowry) in the 1920s. *Buncombe County Special Collections, Pack Memorial Public Library, Asheville, North Carolina.*

inadvertently destroy rare and sensitive plant species, including pinkshell azaleas, while trying to find the site. On June 27, 2023, the wreckage was removed, requiring a helicopter airlift to extract the largest remains.

Looking farther to the east, see if you can spot the white cross atop Mount Lyn Lowry's summit, which has been standing tall since 1964. Myths have evolved over the years to explain why it's there, including one about a girl who got lost near the mountain and her father, who built the cross to guide her home (see *Lyn Lowry's Mountain Memorial* for the true story of the cross's origin).

Plott Balsam's summit rises in the northeast, beyond Mount Lyn Lowry. The story of the girl lost on Mount Lyn Lowry may be a myth, but for others, it became a reality on July 12, 2018.

While attempting to hike an unmaintained trail to Mount Lyn Lowry's summit, a group of teens and young adults became lost. The beer they packed in probably didn't help their sense of direction. Luckily, they had cell reception and were able to call 911. In the dead of night, the group emerged safely from the woods with members of the Haywood County Search and

Rescue team, including this author. The incident serves as a cautionary tale: it's best to stick to the official trails unless you have experience traveling cross-country (and to enjoy libations after your hike).

When you're ready, reverse your route to the junction with the Mountains to Sea Trail and turn left onto it, taking it 2.2 miles back to the Fork Ridge Overlook Trailhead.

LYN LOWRY'S MOUNTAIN MEMORIAL

Mount Lyn Lowry was once Jones Knob, but it was officially renamed in honor of Lyn Lowry, a native of Tampa, Florida, who died from leukemia a month after she turned fifteen in 1962. Her parents, retired army Lieutenant General Sumter Lowry, and her mother, Ivilyn, honored Lyn's legacy by erecting a sixty-foot-tall cross on their property in 1964. The cross was to memorialize their beloved daughter, who loved spending time in the mountains.

General Lowry, an engineer, had gone into the steel industry after fighting in World War I and World War II. He was able to have the fifty-thousand-pound steel cross built and transported in six segments from Jacksonville, Florida, to the mountain. The segments had to be dragged behind a bulldozer near the summit since there were no roads to reach it. Seven mercury vapor bulbs were installed on the cross, and it began illuminating the night sky on August 6, 1964. The lights could be seen from as far as thirty miles away. But it hasn't always been easy to keep it lit.

In 2011, a lightning strike hit the cross, and it remained dark for several months until electrical repairs could be made. Then the original mercury vapor bulbs in the cross were discontinued due to environmental energy regulations, and the carriages for the bulbs were showing their age, too. The family persisted in figuring out solutions, and by 2016, the cross had been rewired and outfitted with LED bulbs.

On August 9, 1965, a year after the cross was erected, Reverend Billy Graham dedicated it.

> *We have tears in our eyes as we miss the loved one who was taken from us. On the other hand, we rejoice that out of her death has come this symbol of the pure and wonderful life she led.*
>
> *—Reverend Billy Graham at the dedication for the cross on Mount Lyn Lowry*

LED bulbs and an overhaul of the electrical system of the cross keep it shining brightly.
Photograph by the author.

By 1970, annual gatherings with gospel singing had begun to occur on a cleared knoll below the cross. The family added a sign to the area that is still present today, coining the knoll, "Mt. Lyn Lowry Singing Grounds." Over the years, the event drew increasingly larger crowds, becoming somewhat of a tourist attraction. As the mountain was subdivided and a gated community evolved, the singings were discontinued.

The Sumter Lowry family established a trust to maintain the cross and the tranquil knoll of the singing grounds, where a small, weathered statue of the Virgin Mary still rests near a covered pavilion; however, it is hemmed in by private, gated property and is no longer accessible to the public.

It's still possible to reach the cross on foot through public lands. The route departs near Waterrock Knob's summit, and you can find trail reports for it online; however, consider yourself warned that the rugged route is not officially maintained, and it traverses through a fragile ecosystem. I don't recommend taking it unless you have strong navigational skills and experience hiking in technical, unsigned terrain.

CONTINUING EDUCATION

Bernstein, Danny. *The Mountains to Sea Trail Across North Carolina: Walking a Thousand Miles Through Wildness, Culture and History*. The History Press, 2013.

Plott, Bob. *The Story of the Plott Hound: Strike and Stay*. The History Press, 2007.

18

MOUNTAINS TO SEA TRAIL

RATTLESNAKE LODGE

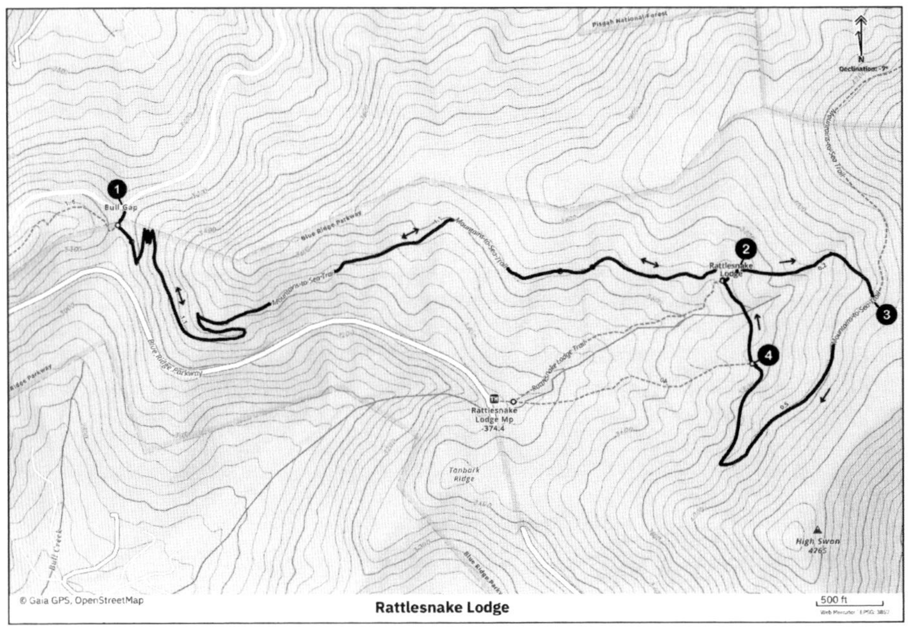

Rattlesnake Lodge

OVERVIEW

If you have a fear of snakes, don't let it deter you from considering this hike. While the name sounds ominous, you are no more likely to encounter a rattlesnake on this hike than anywhere else in Pisgah National Forest. Rattlesnake Lodge, a summer retreat built in 1903 by Dr. Chase P. Ambler, an Asheville-based tuberculosis physician, got its name from the rattlesnake skins that decorated the ceiling of the home's living room. Dr. Ambler reportedly paid five dollars per snake (a week's wages at the time) to anyone who killed the pit vipers on his property. Forty-one snakes were found in the first three years, but Dr. Ambler was known to continue paying the bounty for snakes killed and brought to him from afar.

Despite Dr. Ambler's less-than-friendly attitude toward snakes, he was otherwise an active conservationist and the founder of the Appalachian Mountain Club, which later became the Carolina Mountain Club (CMC) that is still active today. In fact, it is the largest and most active trail organization in the entire region, and CMC trail maintenance volunteers take care of this section of the Mountains to Sea Trail.

THE STATS

Distance: 3.8 miles, lollipop loop
Difficulty: Moderate
Elevation Gain and Loss: 830-foot gain, 812-foot loss
Maps: USGS 7.5' Craggy Pinnacle, National Geographic no. 779 Linville Gorge, Mount Mitchell
Trailhead GPS Coordinates: 35.66977, -82.47127
Highlights: Great winter views, beautiful fall colors, extensive stone ruins of a private summer retreat
Notes: Leashed dogs are allowed. Despite Dr. Ambler's tradition of killing snakes on his property, it is now against federal law to disturb or kill snakes anywhere along this hike.
Driving Directions: From I-240, take exit 4A for U.S. Highway 19/23 north toward Weaverville. In 6 miles, take exit 21 for New Stock Road. Turn right at the end of the ramp, and then take a quick left. Go 0.8 miles, and at the stoplight, turn right onto Reems Creek Road. Go 4 miles and turn right onto Ox Creek Road. In 3.5 miles, there is a small parking area on your left and a bit more parking along the road.

WAYPOINTS

1. Mountains to Sea Trailhead
2. Rattlesnake Lodge ruins (1.3 miles)
3. Mountains to Sea Trail junction (1.7 miles)
4. Chimney remains and junction with Rattlesnake Lodge Trail (2.2 miles)

HIKE DESCRIPTION

The hike starts at Bull Gap on the path in front of the small pullout on Ox Creek Road. (**1**) Bull Gap holds its own history, as it was the last place where either a wild bull buffalo or bull elk was shot in North Carolina in 1799. This was also the spot where Dr. Ambler and his family arrived to visit their retreat. There was once a carriage house at Bull Gap, where horse-drawn carriages were left while the family either walked or rode on horseback to the lodge.

After walking about 150 feet, turn left onto the Mountains to Sea Trail (MST) and look for the round white blazes on the trees to guide you on the well-worn path that terminates on the other side of the state in Jockey's Ridge State Park.

The trail begins with a half-mile ascent on fence-lined switchbacks. Switchbacks are a rarity on trails in southern Appalachia, and they make the climb far more enjoyable than it would be if you went straight up the hillside. Continue climbing through a predominantly hardwood forest punctuated with an occasional evergreen. After 0.7 miles, the views open toward the Swannanoa River valley to the south and Lane Pinnacle's pointed peak to the east as you pass over a large rock face.

Just after hiking one mile, a pair of large boulders flanking the trail are your signal to start looking through the leaf litter for stone remains. In 1.2 miles, they're hard to miss as you walk above one of the most well-preserved foundations on the property—the barn. Dr. Ambler kept cows and horses in his barn, and there was a pigpen just down the hill from it. Take one of the worn paths to stand in front of this well-preserved wall. It was dry constructed, meaning the stones were stacked by hand and do not have concrete to hold them in place.

As you continue your journey back on the main trail, you'll come across the remains of the shallow concrete-walled swimming pool to the right. The pool, only a few feet deep, was gravity fed through an underground aqueduct that led from springs uphill.

Next, you'll arrive at a flat area where the main house once stood with its flat yard stretching before it. There is a worn sign with a brief history of the lodge and photographs of the home and the Ambler family (**2**).

Mrs. Ambler and the children spent their entire summers at the lodge, and Dr. Ambler joined them on the weekends and most Wednesdays. A year-round caretaker lived on the property. It was a constant work in progress, with additional structures being built. The house was built from hand-hewn

The five Ambler children and two others in Rattlesnake Lodge's pool, around 1909. *Buncombe County Special Collections, Pack Memorial Public Library, Asheville, North Carolina.*

chestnut that was cut on the property. Even the furniture in the home was constructed on site with local wood.

The family received guests regularly, and it must have been quite a treat to come enjoy not only the home but also the pool, tennis courts and terraced gardens. The lodge had a bridge that stretched from the second floor to a hill that led to the tennis courts through the gardens.

In 1920, the family sold the home, but it burned six years later, likely from a lightning strike. Eventually, the land became part of the Blue Ridge Parkway's property.

Continuing, you'll quickly pass a blue-blazed trail that leads downhill and to the right, and then you'll arrive at a signed junction with another blue-blazed trail that heads straight ahead and uphill. The remains of the toolshed are in a depression below you. You'll loop back around to this spot on the MST, which continues to the right.

Follow the blue-blazed trail steeply uphill for 0.2 miles until you arrive at the main reservoir for the springhouse. Look for the pipe that's still sticking out of the mossy stone wall. Walk above it to appreciate the size of the entire structure and look for the stone-lined coverless manhole just above it. In another 0.2 miles, you'll arrive at the junction with the MST (**3**). It's easy to spot the rock-lined primary spring coming out of the hillside. Look closely

Rattlesnake Lodge from the front yard, early 1900s. *Buncombe County Special Collections, Pack Memorial Public Library, Asheville, North Carolina.*

and you'll probably be able to find the pipe emerging from it, partially embedded in the damp ground.

Take a right onto the MST and start your downhill journey. Along the way, you'll pass through a tunnel of mountain laurel. At mile 2.2, you'll pass the remains of a chimney (**4**). The Ambler family coined this structure "the shack," and it housed construction workers with bunk beds and a fireplace. Later, it was offered up at no charge to hikers or riders who were passing through en route to Craggy Gardens or Mount Mitchell. There was a water-driven generator nearby that provided electricity to the main home.

When you arrive at the junction where you started hiking up the blue-blazed trail, turn left and retrace your steps on the MST back to the trailhead at Bull Gap.

NORTH CAROLINA'S MOUNTAINS TO SEA TRAIL

September 9, 1977, marked an important day for North Carolina trail lovers. Howard Lee, then the North Carolina secretary of natural resources and community development, proposed "establishing a state trail between the

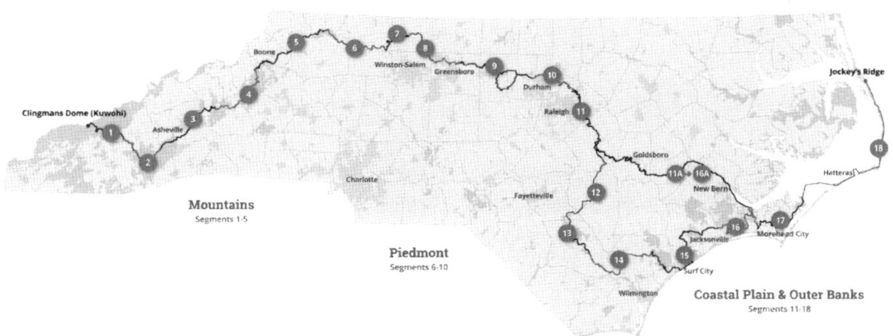

Mountains to Sea Trail map. *Friends of the Mountains to Sea Trail.*

mountains and the seashore in North Carolina." His proposal was inspired by the 1973 North Carolina Trails System Act, which emphasized the need for numerous trails "to provide for the ever-increasing outdoor recreation needs of an expanded population and…promote public access to, travel within, and enjoyment and appreciation of the outdoor, natural, and remote areas of the State."

After the seed was planted, Lee's vision of the future Mountains to Sea Trail (MST) took root in the minds of many; however, connecting existing trails to make a route that spans an entire (and very long) state while building new trails to fill the gaps, all while seeking funding, volunteers and private land rights, doesn't happen overnight. In fact, the MST is still an active work in progress, decades later.

The good news is that in early 2024, about 725 miles of trail exist along the 1,200-mile-long route, stretching from Kuwohi (formerly Clingmans Dome) in Great Smoky Mountains National Park to Jockey's Ridge on the Outer Banks. Temporary routes on back roads and bicycle paths and even an alternate Neuse River paddle route offer a "choose your own adventure" for those who wish to tackle the length of the entire route before it is officially complete.

North Carolina's flagship trail contains a little of everything the state has to offer along its eighteen segments, divided into the Mountain, Piedmont and Coastal Plains and Outer Banks regions. It even presents the opportunity to claim bragging rights for climbing the tallest mountain and tallest sand dune in the eastern United States. To amble along any section of it is to walk through history, and it is a worthwhile endeavor, no matter where you pick it up.

CONTINUING EDUCATION

Barker, Jerry. *Discovering North Carolina's Mountains to Sea Trail: A Companion for Hikers and Armchair Explorers.* University of North Carolina Press, 2024.

Grode, Jim. *Great Day Hikes on North Carolina's Mountains to Sea Trail.* University of North Carolina Press, 2020.

Jester Wallis Productions. "I Am the MST: A Mountains to Sea Trail Documentary." October 8, 2023. YouTube. www.youtube.com.

Above: The Bartram Trail. *Blue Ridge Bartram Trail Conservancy.*

Left: Shuckstack Lookout Tower. *Photo by the author.*

Left: Hickey Fork Falls. *Jordan Mitchell/ Hike WNC.*

Below: Dupont State Forest, Triple Falls. *Photograph by the author.*

Shadow of the Bear on Whiteside Mountain. *Andrew Renfro.*

Cessna wreckage on Browning Knob. *Photograph by the author.*

Springhouse for Buck Springs Lodge. *Photograph by the author.*

Rock House Creek Lodge in Cradle of Forestry. *Photograph by the author.*

Architectural art on the Asheville Urban Trail. *Photograph by the author.*

Backpackers at the Icewater Spring Shelter on the Appalachian Trail. *Christopher Marshburn.*

Goats at the Carl Sandburg National Historic Site. *Photograph by the author.*

A hiker having fun with the cars on Lakeshore Trail. *Steve Dickinson.*

Above: A backpacker on Charlies Bunion. *Adam Williamson/Up N' Adam Adventures.*

Left: Cascades on Laurel Creek. *Misty Gilbert.*

Cook Cabin on Little Cataloochee Trail. *Photograph by the author.*

Hikers getting close to Mount Mitchell's summit on the Black Mountain Crest Trail. *Steven Shattuck.*

Summer mushrooms along the Cataloochee Divide Trail. *Melissa Coatney.*

Waterwheel foundation on Noland Creek. *Photograph by the author.*

Ridgeline Cemetery near Noland Creek Trail. *Photograph by the author.*

Elk on Oconaluftee River Trail. *Photograph by the author.*

The author's husband and dog on the Mountains to Sea Trail under Browning Knob's summit. *Photograph by the author.*

The author's children running toward Purchase Knob. *Photograph by the author.*

Left: Upper Catawba Falls. *Photograph by the author.*

Below: A late-summer view on the Appalachian Trail near the Shuckstack Lookout Tower. *Photograph by the author.*

Turk's Cap Lilies on the Bartram Trail. *Photograph by the author.*

Mount Lyn Lowry's cross. *Photograph by the author.*

Sunset from Yellow Mountain Lookout Tower. *Erin/Adobe Stock.*

Oconaluftee River Trail. *Pat/Adobe Stock.*

View from the Airstrip Trail in Dupont State Forest. *Photograph by the author.*

Hiker lounging on Cold Mountain's summit. *Melissa Coatney.*

Serpentine curves of the Linn Cove Viaduct. *Zack Frank.*

Rattlesnake Lodge barn wall. *Photograph by the author.*

19

TANAWHA TRAIL

LINN COVE VIADUCT

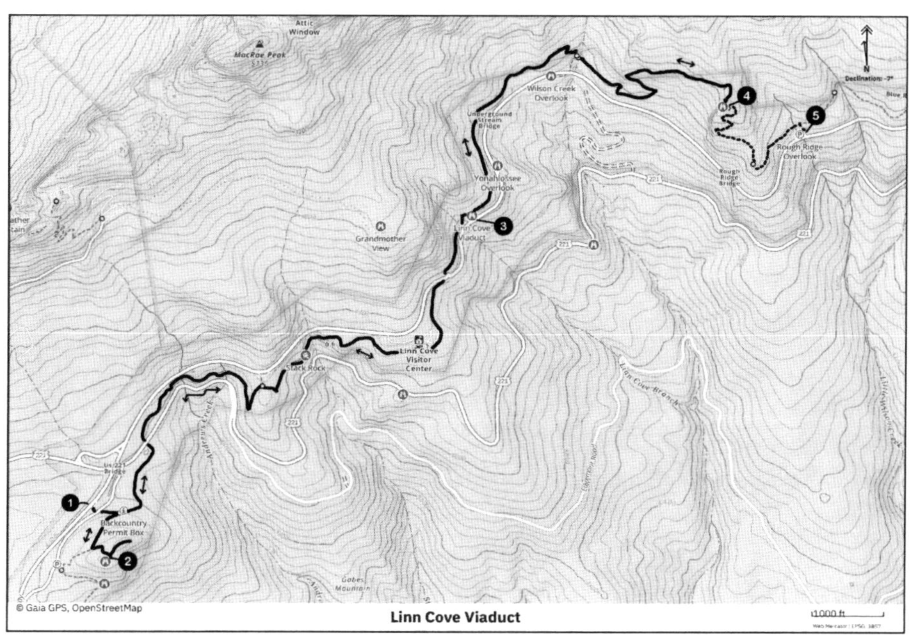

Linn Cove Viaduct

OVERVIEW

The Tanawha Trail, completed in 1993 at the cost of nearly $750,000, stretches 13.5 miles from Julian Price Park to Beacon Heights while paralleling the Blue Ridge Parkway on Grandfather Mountain. Tanawha is the Cherokee word for "fabulous hawk" or "fabulous eagle," and it is the original name of Grandfather Mountain—a fitting tribute for a trail that soars and dips along the contours of the iconic 5,964-foot-tall massif. Today, you'll traverse the first few miles of this trail, taking you beside and beneath the Linn Cove Viaduct. It's the Blue Ridge Parkway's most famous and photographed bridge, and you've likely seen it in photographs of the iconic roadway without realizing it had a name and fascinating history.

If you're concerned this hike highlights only man-made marvels, don't worry; the route also travels through a wide range of interesting terrain and a fragile and ancient ecosystem, passing beside Stack Rock and leading you to several jaw-dropping vistas. The Mountains to Sea Trail, which spans from Kuwohi (formerly Clingmans Dome) in Great Smoky Mountains National Park to Jockey's Ridge State Park on the North Carolina coast, piggybacks the Tanawha Trail, so you'll be able to claim bragging rights for hiking a portion of both trails by the day's end.

THE STATS

Distance: 7 miles (or about 4.6 miles if completed as a one-way shuttle hike)
Difficulty: Difficult
Elevation Gain and Loss: 870-foot gain, 870-foot loss
Maps: National Geographic no. 779 Pisgah National Forest—Linville Gorge, Mount Mitchell; USGS 7.5' Grandfather Mountain
Trailhead GPS Coordinates: 36.08389, -81.83018
Highlights: Linn Cove Viaduct, an ancient ecosystem, sweeping views, enormous rock formations
Notes: Seasonal restrooms are located at the Linn Cove Visitor Center. Leashed dogs are allowed. Check for road closures on the Blue Ridge Parkway, especially in winter. Always stay on the trail to protect the fragile environment. This trail can also be hiked as a one-way shuttle hike (see the following section for details).
Driving Directions: Drive to the paved parking area at milepost 304 on the Blue Ridge Parkway. To complete the one-way shuttle hike option, leave another car at the parking area at milepost 302.8. If you opt for the one-way shuttle hike, consider hiking the route in the opposite direction—from Rough Ridge to Beacon Heights—if you prefer a more downhill hike.

WAYPOINTS

1. Tanawha Trail Trailhead
2. Beacon Heights summit (0.3 mile)
3. Linn Cove Viaduct (2.1 miles)
4. Rough Ridge overlook (3.5 miles)
5. Rough Ridge parking area for one-way shuttle hike (4.6 miles)

HIKE DESCRIPTION

The hike begins at the Tanawah Trail's southern terminus, which it shares with the path to Beacon Heights, whose summit boasts a pair of can't-miss, weathered, broad rock outcrops with gorgeous views (**1**). Just beyond the trailhead parking area and on the same side of the parkway, you'll immediately cross Carroll Gragg Road to reach the trail.

Shortly after starting the trail, you'll arrive at a junction. Tanawha Trail continues to the left, while Beacon Heights Trail veers to the right. The quick detour to summit Beacon Heights is worthwhile, so turn right and climb a third of a mile through rocky terrain choked with rhododendron to arrive at the summit with two viewpoints. Your efforts will be rewarded with stunning views, including those of Linville Gorge, Mount Mitchell, Table Rock Mountain, Hawksbill and Grandfather Mountain (**2**).

Retrace your steps back to the junction with the Tanawha Trail and begin following its white feather-shaped blazes. At 0.9 miles, cross over Highway 221 and continue the trail as it parallels the Blue Ridge Parkway through a forest filled with lush greenery like galax, which emits a pungent onion-like smell; ferns; moss-covered rocks; and rhododendron. At the 1-mile mark, you'll walk beside an enormous stone retaining wall, which was built for the parkway above you.

Around 1.4 miles, you'll pass a spur trail on the left, which leads to Stack Rock Overlook on the parkway. Continue straight toward Stack Rock on the Tanawaha Trail, and you'll soon ascend and then descend wooden stairs that wrap around the impressive tower of stacked boulders. A wooden bridge leads the way across the aptly named Stack Rock Creek before it takes you up another flight of stairs, this time made of wood and stone.

Just after the two-mile mark, you'll arrive at Linn Cove Visitor Center, which has seasonal bathrooms. Your feet will get a temporary reprieve from

the rough trail terrain as you traverse a paved stretch of trail, created for wheelchair accessibility.

After you pass through the parking area, the trail descends beneath the colossal viaduct so you can witness its underbelly (**3**). The seams between the concrete sections are easy to discern, and one of the seven footings along the length of the quarter-mile viaduct is front and center, only its footprint disturbing the ground beneath it.

Next, the rocky, root-covered trail ascends stone steps as it passes an impressive rock wall. It's slow going through this more technical section. Take your time and appreciate the work that went into creating this special trail and the viaduct. Finally, the trail levels off in an area dominated by beech and birch trees. You are now walking parallel to the viaduct, and you can catch several nearly eye-level views of it to the right of the trail and through the tree canopy. The trail descends again as it approaches the Wilson Creek drainage and the bridge that spans its rocky bed a little past the three-mile mark.

Beyond Wilson Creek, the trail passes through a boulder field that is full of much larger rock formations, and it starts climbing in earnest toward the aptly named Rough Ridge (**4**). Stone steps lead the way to the ridge, situated at 4,750 feet, the highest point on this hike. Anchored cables will guide you to the various viewing points if you wish to explore beyond the first rocky perch. It's a magnificent place to witness the viaduct from above, as well as Hawksbill, Table Rock and Grandfather Mountain. Below where you

Opposite: Linn Cove Viaduct from the Tanawha Trail. *Photograph by the author.*

Above: View from Rough Ridge looking toward the Linn Cove Viaduct. *Photograph by the author.*

stand on Rough Ridge is one of the South's most popular rock climbing sites called Ship Rock, where climbers often enjoy the rocky face. Once you've spent adequate time on Rough Ridge, retrace your steps nearly four miles from where you started.

ONE-WAY SHUTTLE HIKE OPTION

If you're hiking the one-way shuttle option, continue another 0.6 miles on the Tanawha Trail from Rough Ridge to the Rough Ridge parking area at mile marker 302.8 (**5**).

THE LINN COVE VIADUCT HISTORY

The construction of the Blue Ridge Parkway started in 1935, but the building of its last section, the Linn Cove Viaduct, didn't begin until

1979, when Congress finally approved the funding. This "missing link" of the parkway brought its fair share of controversy over the years, largely stemming from where the road would fit best around Grandfather Mountain in relation to private ownership of the surrounding area, including the Mile-High Swinging Bridge. While it would appear to many that environmental concerns about this ancient and fragile landscape played a significant role in the process, as outlined in *Super-Scenic Motorway: A Blue Ridge Parkway History*, the decision "had more to do with maintaining longtime Parkway aesthetics of preserving scenery and minimizing scar than with a science-based environmental concern about the flora and fauna of Grandfather Mountain."

Ultimately, engineers from the Federal Highway Administration (FHA) and landscape architects from the National Park Service (NPS) conceived the idea of creating a viaduct. According to the NPS website, "Viaducts are elevated roadway sections carrying the road high above dry ravines or across the shoulders of mountains where extensive and aesthetically unpleasing fill sections would otherwise be required." The Linn Cove Viaduct would become the most famous and longest of such roadway sections on the

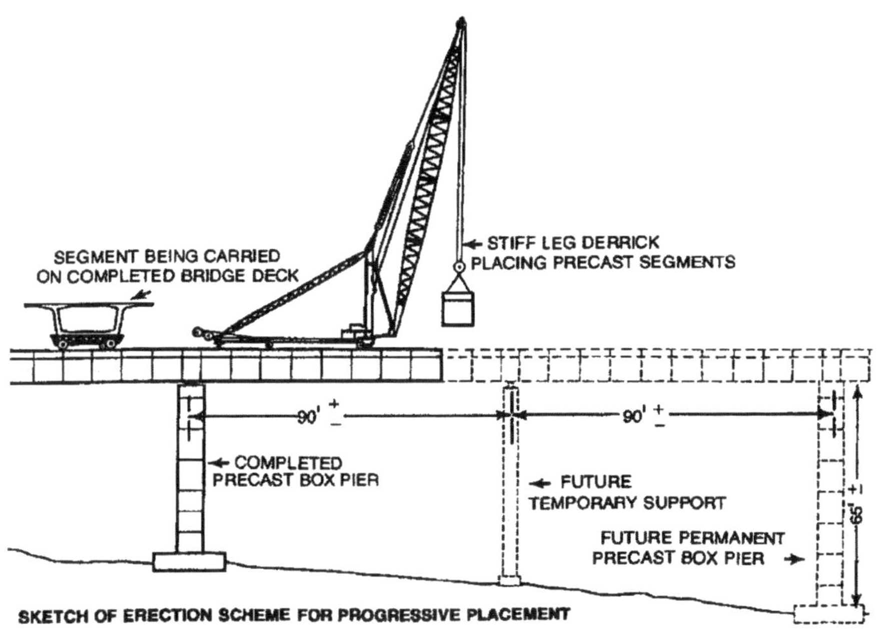

Diagram of the Linn Cove Viaduct from the National Park Service Historic American Engineering Record NC-42-A. *National Park Service.*

469-mile-long Blue Ridge Parkway. Figg and Muller Engineers Inc. took these conceptual ideas from the FHA and NPS and turned them into reality, thoughtfully and meticulously designing one of the most complicated bridges ever built to preserve the integrity of Grandfather Mountain's environment.

First, 153 pre-cast concrete sections, each weighing fifty tons, were made indoors off site, using a process called "match casting," which meant each new segment was cast against the preceding segment. Only the southernmost segment is completely straight; the rest are curved, hugging the mountain slope's contours. Next, so as not to damage the mountainside by building an additional access road to construct the viaduct, each pre-cast section was lowered by a stiff leg crane and epoxied into position against the preceding segment, a process known as "progressive placement." For additional security of the bridge deck, steel cables were threaded through the segments. This was the first time this technique, developed in 1972, was used in the United States.

Seven permanent footings were constructed at ground level, and it was the only part of the process that didn't use the top-down method. Exposed rock in the area was covered to prevent staining from construction materials, such as epoxy, grout and concrete, which was tinted with iron oxide to blend in with nearby rock. Even the trees that were removed beneath the viaduct were individually considered before they were felled. The final cost of the viaduct was $9,863,384.

You can't walk on top of the 1,243-foot length of the Linn Cove Viaduct, since there's no shoulder, but it's a thrill to drive its serpentine curves and marvel at this enormous feat of engineering beside the rugged contours of Grandfather Mountain. It's even more meaningful to contrast the driving experience by walking beneath it on the rugged and rocky Tanawha Trail, whose beauty was protected in the viaduct's creation.

CONTINUING EDUCATION

Whisnant, Anne Mitchell. *Super-Scenic Motorway: A Blue Ridge Parkway History.* University of North Carolina Press, 2010.

PART III

NANTAHALA NATIONAL FOREST

20

BARTRAM TRAIL

CHEOAH BALD

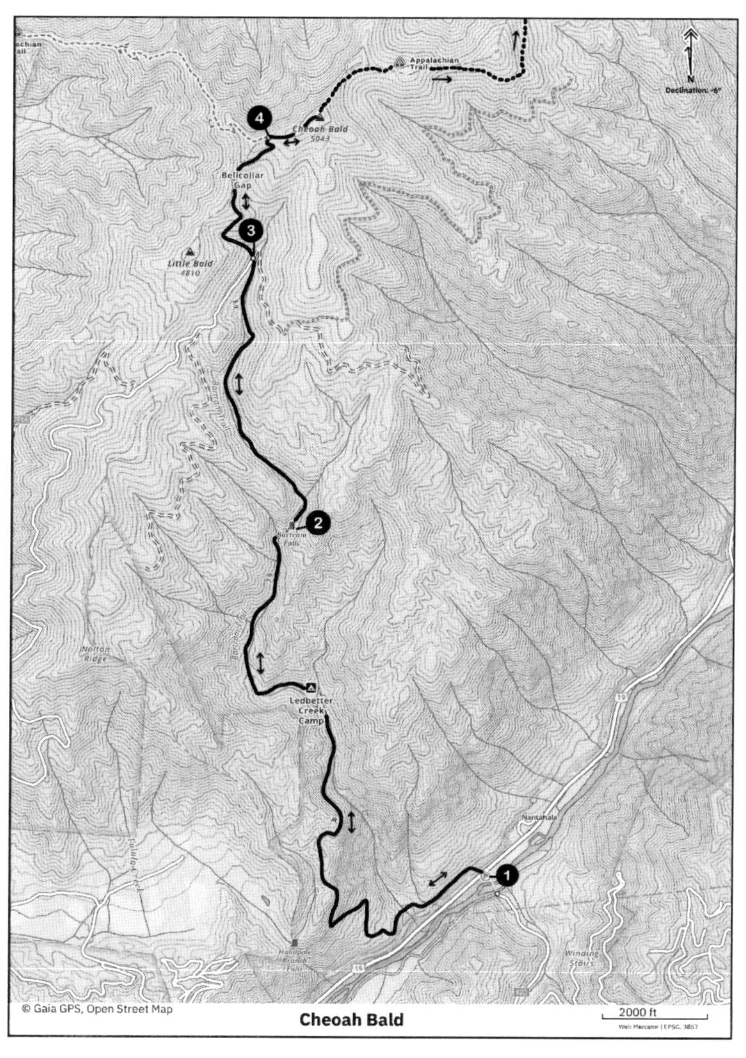

OVERVIEW

Standing at 5,062 feet, Cheoah Bald is hardly the tallest peak in Western North Carolina; however, it does hold this distinction for the Cheoah Mountain Range, rising sharply and nearly 3,000 feet above the Nantahala River Gorge. It is also the northern terminus of the Bartram Trail, which is named after eighteenth-century naturalist William Bartram. When Bartram arrived at the "most elevated peak" of the nearby Nantahala Mountains, he "beheld with rapture and astonishment, a sublimely awful scene of power and magnificence, a world of mountains piled upon mountains." It's hard not to feel the same way at Cheoah's summit.

There are three directions from which one can reach the summit; however, the hike in this chapter is the shortest and arguably the most scenic, if not the toughest. Don't let that deter you if you're up for the challenge. This route is a treasure from spring through fall. In keeping with the trail's namesake botanist, you can count on a wide variety of wildflowers and mushrooms to distract you from the long climb, as well as the beauty of trailside Bartram Falls. The summit is worth the sweat equity, too, greeting visitors with long-range views to the south.

There is also a one-way shuttle option for this hike, continuing on the Appalachian Trail from Cheoah's summit and ending at the famed Nantahala Outdoor Center (NOC), where hearty riverside, post-trail dining options and whitewater entertainment await you. Even if you hike this route as an out-and-back endeavor, I recommend visiting the NOC as part of the adventure.

THE STATS

Distance: 10 miles out and back (or 13 miles as a one-way shuttle hike)
Difficulty: Most Difficult
Elevation Gain and Loss: 3,361-foot gain, 3,361-foot loss
Maps: National Geographic no. 784 Fontana and Hiwassee Lakes; USGS 7.5' Hewitt
Trailhead GPS Coordinates: 35.28509, -83.67009
Highlights: Abundant wildflowers and mushrooms, Bartram Falls, expansive summit views, solitude
Notes: Leashed dogs are allowed. This trail can be combined with the Appalachian Trail to create a one-way shuttle hike to Nantahala Outdoor

Center (see the following section for details). There is significant elevation gain and loss on this hike, so allow a full day to hike it.

Driving Directions: From the Nantahala Outdoor Center on U.S. Highway 19/74, head west for 6.6 miles. Turn left onto Forest Service Road 422 (Winding Stairs), and the parking area is immediately on the right.

WAYPOINTS

1. Bartram Trail Trailhead
2. Bartram Falls (3.0 miles)
3. FR295A junction (4.3 miles)
4. Appalachian Trail junction (4.8 miles)

HIKE DESCRIPTION

To begin the hike, cross U.S. Highway 19/74 and look for the trail that heads into the woods (**1**). In summer, you may need to wade through a small section of overgrowth for the first quarter mile as you travel near the railroad tracks.

After the first 0.4 miles, the trail veers down and to the left, and shortly thereafter, you'll pass an established campsite and cross Ledbetter Creek on a footbridge. Soon after, the trail begins climbing steeply for over a mile. At 1.4 miles, it levels out temporarily through a rhododendron tunnel before it makes a second and unbridged crossing of Ledbetter Creek. This second crossing is usually an easy rock-hop, but the crossings ahead may require you to get your feet wet, depending on water levels.

At the three-mile mark, Bartram Falls comes into view on the right (**2**). You can easily view the cataract from the trail, but it's not safe to descend the slope to get closer (and it doesn't improve the view). As you continue climbing, now more gently, you'll pass another interesting series of cascades, where the water of Ledbetter Creek is funneled through channels formed by large rectangular stones covered in vibrant green moss. This unique sluiceway is as interesting as Bartram Falls. Take a few minutes to study the angles the rocks create and observe how the water rushes through them to find its way to the falls.

Around 3.5 miles in, the terrain loosens its grip as you pass through an open cove, the creek singing merrily beside you. In another mile, you'll cross a footbridge over Ledbetter Creek and continue through one of the lushest

Bartram Falls cascading down Cheoah Bald's slopes. *Photograph by the author.*

Sweeping views from Cheoah Bald's summit. *Photograph by the author.*

sections of the trail. At 4.3 miles, the trail crosses over FR 295A at an angle. It resumes a steep ascent, leaving the Ledbetter Creek watershed while climbing toward Bellcollar Gap (**3**).

At mile 4.8, you'll reach the signed T-junction with the Appalachian Trail and turn right, still heading uphill but less steeply (**4**). In another .25 miles, you'll arrive at the summit of Cheoah Bald, where there's a wooden sign nailed to a tree. The 180-degree views to the southeast boast multiple mountain ranges within Nantahala National Forest, and the conical summit of Wayah Bald to the far left is the most recognizable.

Cheoah Bald was first called Sehwate-yi, or the "Hornet Place." According to Eastern Cherokee legend, a giant hornet used this summit and nearby Swim Bald for its nest. The angry hornet was often spotted sunbathing on the bald. If anyone came near the mountain, the hornet would drive them away.

From the summit, retrace your steps back to the trailhead unless you've opted for the one-way shuttle hike, which ends at Nantahala Outdoor Center (described in the following section and marked with a dashed line on this chapter's map).

ONE-WAY SHUTTLE HIKE OPTION

From Cheoah Bald's summit, continue following the Appalachian Trail for eight more miles, ending your hike at the Nantahala Outdoor Center (NOC). Shuttles for this option can be self-managed, but you can also inquire about shuttling services through the Blue Ridge Bartram Trail Conservancy's website (www.blueridgebartram.org).

WILLIAM BARTRAM: FATHER OF AMERICAN BOTANY

Long before backpackers began schlepping lightweight modern gear to walk the distance of footpaths like the Appalachian Trail, an early pioneer and wilderness preservationist, William Bartram, traveled a 2,400-mile route on horseback, by boat and on foot. From 1773 to 1777, he visited what would become the Southeastern United States (then colonial), exploring parts of Florida, Georgia, Alabama, Louisiana and the Carolinas. The 114-mile Bartram Trail, a designated National Recreational Trail that spans from Cheoah Bald to Russell Bridge in Georgia, was first conceived by the late

Brevard-based landscape architect Walter G. McKelvey in the 1970s and follows part of Bartram's route.

Vivid journal entries and illustrations from Bartram's four-year journey were published in book form in 1791 (*Travels with William Bartram*), and the lyrical account is still in print. Bartram provided some of the only known written documentation of Native customs and villages in the region during the time of his travels, and he formed amicable relationships with the tribes he encountered. He was given the nickname "Puc Puggy" by the Muskogeans, which translates to "the flower hunter"—a fitting moniker because Bartram meticulously documented and illustrated over two hundred native plant species previously unknown to Western civilization during his four-year sojourn.

NANTAHALA OUTDOOR CENTER

The NOC, founded in 1972 by a group of nature-loving friends, had more humble origins than the outdoor giant it has become would suggest. It started as a small motel and gas station. Payson Kennedy, one of the NOC founders, played a stunt double in the Academy Award–winning film *Deliverance* in 1971. After the movie's release, whitewater rafting surged in popularity. The NOC strategically offered trips on the Chattooga River, where the movie was filmed, and along the Nantahala River.

Nowadays, outdoor enthusiasts can choose from over 120 land- and water-based activities from one of the NOC's ten locations that span four states. Appalachian Trail thru hikers especially look forward to visiting the original location, since the trail weaves through the heart of the property. Twenty-three Olympians, including two gold medalists, have trained on the Nantahala River at the original NOC location, and it is one of the most active paddle sports event venues in the country.

Despite its growth, the original Nantahala River NOC campus has maintained some of the old-school outdoor charm that put it on the map. It's a memorable place to visit, and it's especially fun to "paddle watch" from one of its dining venues.

CONTINUING EDUCATION

Bartram, William. *William Bartram: Travels and Other Writings*. Travels of America, 1996.
Martin, Brent. *The Changing Blue Ridge Mountains: Essay on Journeys Past and Present*. The History Press, 2019.
Martin, Brent. *A Hiker's Guide to The Bartram National Recreation Trail in Georgia and North Carolina*. Milestone Press, 2024.

21

JOYCE KILMER MEMORIAL FOREST LOOP

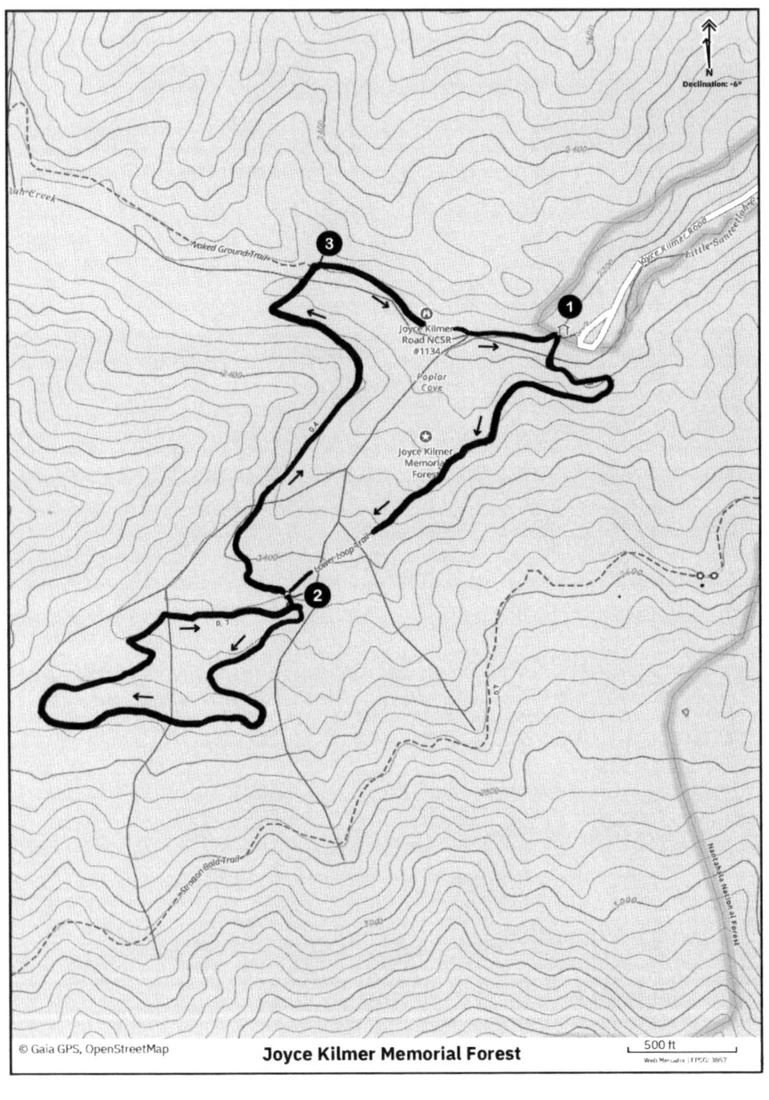

OVERVIEW AND HISTORY

This forest memorial, named after poet and World War I veteran Joyce Kilmer, leaves an indelible imprint on its visitors, partly due to the enormous evidence (literally) of the absence of logging in the area. Lumber companies that purchased the land initially deemed the steep, rugged landscape too inhospitable for timber transport via waterways. The Great Depression likely exacerbated the situation, causing a decline in lumber prices.

In 1936, the U.S. Forest Service purchased 13,055 acres from the Gennett Lumber Company for the astronomical price of twenty-eight dollars per acre (at a time when most land was selling for three to four dollars per acre). Later, 3,800 acres were dedicated as the Joyce Kilmer Memorial Forest in response to the New York chapter of the Veterans for Foreign Wars proposing a living tribute in Kilmer's memory.

This hike will lead you into one of the largest contiguous tracts of old-growth forests in the eastern United States, home to trees that are over four hundred years old, some with circumferences exceeding twenty feet. Your neck may be sore by the end of your hike after craning to look for the canopies of these giants. Though the hike is short, you'll want ample time to meander among these giants.

THE STATS

Distance: 1.9-mile, figure-eight loop
Difficulty: Easy
Elevation Gain and Loss: 351-foot gain, 351-foot loss
Maps: National Geographic no. 784 Nantahala National Forest—Fontana and Hiwassee Lakes; USGS 7.5' Santeelah Creek
Trailhead GPS Coordinates: 35.35906, -83.92839
Highlights: Enormous trees, a spectacular display of spring wildflowers
Notes: Restrooms and picnic tables are available at the trailhead. Leashed dogs are allowed.
Driving Directions: From Robbinsville, take Highway 129 north for 1.5 miles to the junction with Highway 143 West (Massey Branch Road). Turn left on Highway 143 and travel 5 miles to a stop sign. Turn right onto Kilmer Road. Drive for 7.3 miles and bear right at the junction of Santeetlah Gap and Cherohala Skyway. In 2.5 miles, you will find the entrance of the Joyce Kilmer Memorial Forest.

WAYPOINTS

1. Lower Loop Trailhead
2. Upper Loop junction (0.5 miles)
3. Naked Ground Trail junction (1.6 miles)

HIKE DESCRIPTION

The 3,800-acre Joyce Kilmer–Slickrock Wilderness has a reputation for housing some of the most rugged and strenuous trails in Western North Carolina. This hike, however, doesn't require nearly as much effort as the trails surrounding it. It receives droves of foot traffic each year, and priority is placed on maintaining it for casual hikers.

The Cherokee originally inhabited this pristine acreage, but in the 1700s, half the population (around four hundred people) died from smallpox. The John Denton family are the only recorded white settlers to have lived in what is now the memorial forest. John and Albertine Denton had five children, and their oldest child, Charles, was born in a Benton, Tennessee jailhouse, where they lived at the time. In 1879, the family moved from Tennessee and built a six-room cabin with two chimneys. The cabin was so well constructed that the U.S. Forest Service had to dismantle it with dynamite. While he built their permanent residence, John transformed a nearby fallen chestnut tree into a lean-to temporary home, since he could stand up inside it after he hollowed it out.

This route is a double loop, and the spring that supplied water to the Denton family is about seventy-five yards from the picnic area. From the parking area, just past the information signboard and covered pavilion, you'll cross a footbridge over Little Santeetlah Creek as it rushes toward Santeetlah Lake (**1**). As you continue, you'll ascend several switchbacks with thick vegetation on the slope beside you. This area is a mecca for those who love spring wildflowers.

You'll cross more small streams on footbridges that run over the trail and ascend a series of wooden steps, eventually reaching the first old-growth trees of the hike—yellow birch and beech. If the size of these trees doesn't impress you, just wait.

At the half-mile mark, the upper loop portion of the hike begins (**2**). At this junction, a plaque memorializing Joyce Kilmer awaits. Proceed into Poplar Cove on the upper part of the loop and prepare to be awed. I

Denton family cabin. *University of North Carolina Asheville.*

recommend hiking the upper loop in a clockwise direction to witness the most impressive trees from the best angles. While you're completing the loop, abide by "leave no trace" principles—leave only footprints and take only memories. It's especially frustrating to discover carvings in a tree that has survived this long, so resist any temptation, and enjoy Mother Nature's exquisite artwork as it is.

Within this forest, some of the most impressive species include Carolina silver bells, red oaks and basswoods; however, it's the *Liriodendron tulipifera* that steal the show. Over time, botanical species take on multiple common names, and this species is no exception. *Liriodendron tulipifera* is a part of the magnolia family of trees, and if you've ever seen their large flowers blooming in spring, the name "tulipifera" will make a lot of sense. Most people refer to these trees as tulip poplars or yellow poplars. While on this hike, I think it's safe to simply refer to them as "stunning" and to replace scientific nomenclature with awe.

There won't be any question if you've found one of the giant tulip trees, but you'll also pass many smaller trees. Over time, old-growth forests become a mixture of new and old growth as old trees die and fall, creating gaps in

Enormous tulip trees in Joyce Kilmer Memorial Forest. *Jordan Mitchell/Hike WNC.*

the canopy for seeds to take root. Just under a mile into the hike, the trail passes right beside one of these fallen giants. The enormous stump has a gaping maw large enough to walk through and stand inside. Imagine the thunderous boom the nearby trunk must have made as it hit the earth.

At 1.2 miles, you will complete the upper loop. Stay to the left to complete the lower loop, which is still a lovely walk through the ancient woods. Cross the stream that drains from Poplar Cove, providing lifeblood to its residents. You'll descend wooden steps to Little Santeelah Creek and cross a second bridge. Naked Ground Trail veers to the left, but stay on the path to the right (**3**). Ascend a flight of stairs built into the slope before making your final descent back to the trailhead.

JOYCE KILMER

Though his life was cut short in World War I, Alfred Joyce Kilmer left a lasting and honorable imprint on the world in his brief thirty-one years. The simple yet heartfelt expression of the wonders of nature and faith in his

Joyce Kilmer in uniform during his service in the 165th Infantry Regiment, 1918. *Library of Congress.*

well-known poem "Trees" is what most people associate him with, but Kilmer achieved a great deal more than only authoring a famous poem.

"Trees" was first published in the August 1913 edition of *Poetry: A Magazine of Verse.* Many towns claimed that Kilmer wrote the poem while visiting them; however, Aline, his widow, wrote in a letter dated March 25, 1929, "The poem, I definitely remember, was written at home, in the afternoon, in the intervals of some writings."

Joyce Kilmer was born in 1886 in New Jersey. His father, Frederick Kilmer, held the unique distinction of inventing Johnson and Johnson's baby powder (long before the company knew the product was occasionally contaminated with asbestos). Writing became a passion for Kilmer an early age, and he was the editor of his grammar school's newspaper.

He proceeded to attend Rutgers College and Columbia University and then married Aline Murray, with whom he had five children. The couple's fourth child, Rose, tragically succumbed to polio at a young age, just before Kilmer left to go overseas and fight in World War I. In addition to his poetry, Kilmer was a literary critic, journalist and editor, writing for publications such as *The New York Times.* He also published several books.

Kilmer was known as a brave and dedicated soldier, and he was not averse to dangerous reconnaissance missions. Sergeant Major Ester, a fellow soldier in World War I, was especially inspired by Kilmer's courage.

> *He would always be doing more than his orders called for, i.e., getting much nearer to the enemy's positions than any officer would be inclined to send him. Night after night he would lie out in No Man's Land, crawling through barbed wires, in an effort to locate enemy positions and enemy guns, and tearing his clothes to shreds.*
>
> —*Sergeant Major Ester*

Kilmer was killed in combat by a German sniper on July 30, 1918, during the Second Battle of the Marne and was buried in France. Posthumously, he was awarded the Croix de Guerre, a French military decoration awarded to individuals for their gallant action in war. In addition to this memorial forest, eight schools, an army camp and several parks and roads are named for Kilmer. New York City's Central Park even houses a monument in his honor. Although Kilmer never stood among these regal giants, his granddaughter proudly represented him during the forest's dedication ceremony on July 30, 1936.

"Trees"
I think that I shall never see
A poem lovely as a tree.
A tree whose hungry mouth is prest
Against the earth's sweet flowing breast;
A tree that looks at God all day,
And lifts her leafy arms to pray;
A tree that may in Summer wear
A nest of robins in her hair;
Upon whose bosom snow has lain;
Who intimately lives with rain.
Poems are made by fools like me,
But only God can make a tree

Joyce Kilmer

CONTINUING EDUCATION

Kilmer, Joyce. *Trees and Other Poems*. CreateSpace, 2017.
Warren, Mark. *Wild Plants and Survival Lore: Secrets of the Forest*. Vol. 1. Lyons Press, 2020.

22

WHITESIDE MOUNTAIN

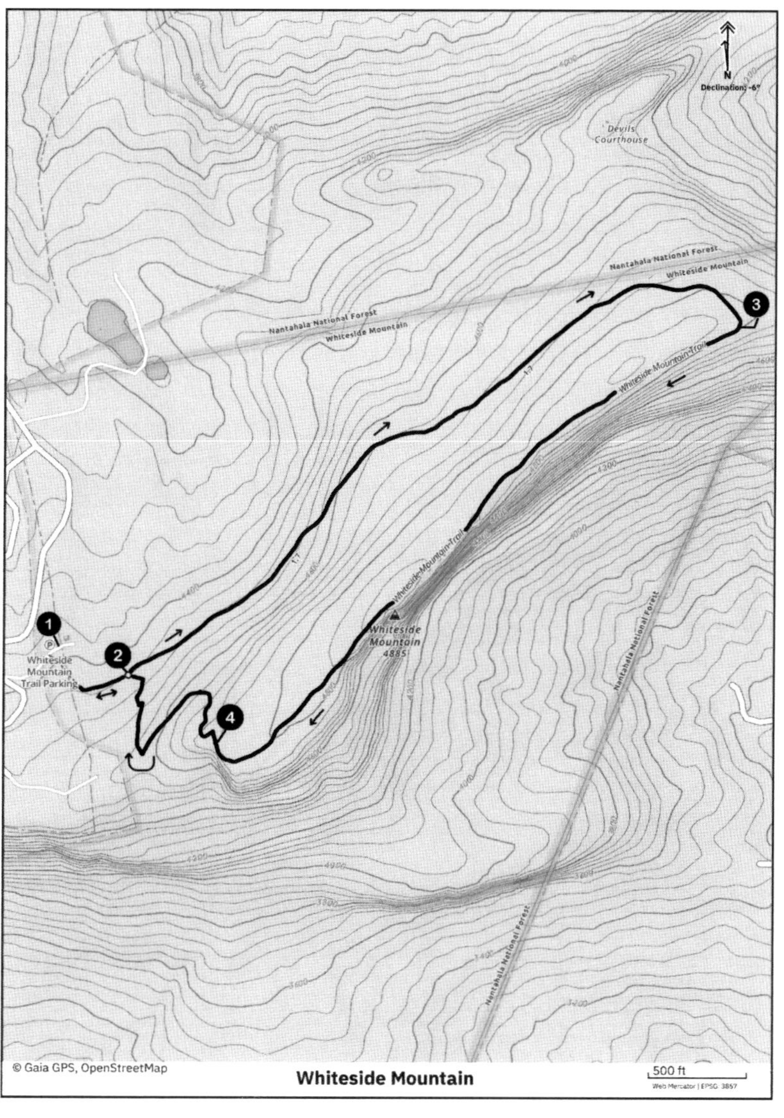

OVERVIEW

Whiteside Mountain, located between Cashiers and Highlands, is considered one of the oldest mountains in the world, with an estimated age of 390 to 460 million years. It is a pluton, which means it's composed of igneous rock, a product of volcanic activity beneath the Earth's surface. The term *pluton* is fittingly derived from Pluto, the Roman god of the underworld. Whiteside Mountain, named for its sheer 750-foot-tall white cliffs, some of the tallest in the East, is a recognizable landmark in Nantahala National Forest. Up to five states can be seen from its summit on a clear day.

This 2-mile popular lollipop loop trail leads you to the massif's 4,930-foot-tall summit with breathtaking views to the east, south and west along the southern summit cliffs. There are plenty of cabled railings for safety, so don't let a fear of heights deter you from experiencing this jewel of a hike.

THE STATS

Distance: 2-mile loop
Difficulty: Moderate
Elevation Gain and Loss: 427-foot gain, 410-foot loss
Maps: National Geographic no. 229 Nantahala and Cullasaja Gorges; USGS 7.5' Highlands
Trailhead GPS Coordinates: 35.08047, -83.14406
Highlights: Panoramic views, spring wildflowers, fall foliage
Notes: A three dollar parking fee may be paid on site or in advance at www.recreation.gov. Restrooms, trash receptacles and picnic tables are available at the trailhead. Leashed dogs are allowed. This trail is family-friendly, but keep a close eye on children.
Driving Directions: From U.S. 64 and NC-107 in Cashiers, follow U.S. 64 east for 4.7 miles. Turn left onto Whiteside Mountain Road (State Road 1600). Follow for 0.9 miles to the signed parking area on the left.

WAYPOINTS

1. Whiteside Mountain Trailhead
2. veer left (0.1 miles)
3. trail levels off and veers right (0.9 miles)
4. start descending steeply (1.5 miles)

HIKE DESCRIPTION

Like many areas in Western North Carolina, Whiteside Mountain and the surrounding forest was impacted by logging in the latter half of the 1800s. Near the end of the century, the mountain and much of the surrounding land was purchased by Prioleau Ravenel Jr. and his mother, Margaretta, when the area became a popular summer destination for the wealthy.

Ravenel died in 1940, and his second wife, Beatrice, inherited the mountain. She sold over 1,500 acres in 1943 to Powell Lumber Company and Champion Paper and Fibre Company. Thankfully, decades earlier, in 1914, the U.S. Forest Service had purchased over 700 acres for $7.50 per acre at the base of the mountain to protect the headwaters of North Mill Creek and Chattooga River. But even so, by 1946, much of the area had been decimated by these lumber companies, and the rivers ran brown with silt because of the intensive logging.

In a span of two years, the lumber companies exhausted the natural resources for which they purchased the land and sought a buyer. The U.S. Forest Service wasn't able to purchase it, since Congress couldn't provide the funding. Instead, the land was sold to Whiteside Mountain Inc., which ran tours to the summit in a Jeep that towed small canopy-covered trailers for a fee of twenty-five cents per person (plus a one dollar toll that allowed access to the parking lot and a concession stand).

This hike initially traverses the same path the tours once did. Thankfully, the land has recovered well from the logging and tour days, but you may feel as though a tram-load of tourists is with you. While the trail can be busy on nice days, it's worth the shared company.

From the parking lot (**1**), you'll ascend 0.1 miles on steps before you reach a junction. Then you'll veer left to begin the loop portion of the hike (**2**) and join the wide, rocky path the tourist bus once traveled. Blasted, moss-covered bluffs and granite dominate the landscape to your right as you ascend. If you're visiting in spring, abundant wildflowers add a splash of color to the forest floor. In summer, blooming rhododendron take center stage, and then yellow birch and maple trees take their turn to show off in the fall. Even winter brings its gifts (and likely less crowds) when impressive ice formations are often found clinging to the rocks.

At 0.9 miles, the trail levels off and a short spur trail to the left will lead you to your first expansive view into the upper Chattanooga River valley and the cliffs of Timber Ridge beyond (**3**). A prominent rocky landmark on the massif, Devils Courthouse, is slightly northeast of where you stand. Just

A George Masa photograph of Whiteside Mountain, probably taken in the 1920s. *Buncombe County Special Collections, Pack Memorial Public Library, Asheville, North Carolina.*

ahead on the trail, there is a railed viewpoint that overlooks Georgia and South Carolina to your south. From this overlook, you'll rejoin the trail and as it begins its traverse along the south slope of Whiteside Mountain.

Views are abundant as you traverse the summit ridge, and the forest service has installed cables for your safety. Be on the lookout in spring and summer for peregrine falcons flying overhead or resting on rock outcrops. The falcon was reintroduced to the mountain in 1985 through the endangered species program. One of the world's fastest bird species, they return annually to nest on rock ledges. Climbing routes are closed during the nesting season, usually from January to June.

Be sure to stop at the interpretive signboard at the aptly named Fools Rock, a protruding granite tongue that projects parallel to the mountain's wall in a tapering fashion, roughly resembling an arrowhead. The sign details a harrowing rescue effort that took place on May 14, 1911. Charles Wright, a local resident, bravely put his life in danger to rescue his friend Gus Baty, who had fallen off Fool's Rock while staging a fall to impress Irene Edwards, a woman who was hiking with the men.

After tumbling over fifty feet, Baty's fall was halted by a small rhododendron that was growing from a crevice and snagged his clothing. This lucky catch spared Baty from spilling over the edge of an 1,800-foot-tall drop just beyond it. Wright, along with Will Dillard, another friend on the hike, precariously made their way to Baty. Dillard eventually halted his efforts for fear of slipping, but Wright stayed the course and reached his friend, who was badly injured and barely conscious. It took over three harrowing hours for Wright to reach Baty and then drag him back to Whiteside's summit (Dillard was eventually able to assist him again), where the rest of their party was waiting. A makeshift litter was constructed, and Baty was carried down the mountain on it.

Five months after this event, a story about the rescue in *The Charlotte Observer* quoted Wright and Dillard as saying that no amount of money could tempt them to undertake the rescue again; however, Wright modified his statement and admitted, "But I guess I would try it if someone was hanging there and I thought I could save his life." The mark of a true hero.

Following the publication of the story in the *Observer*, Wright was awarded the gold Carnegie Medal, a medallion "awarded to civilians who risk death

Whiteside Mountain summit ridge. *Photograph by the author.*

or serious physical injury to an extraordinary degree saving or attempting to save the lives of others," and Dillard was awarded a silver Carnegie Medal. Both awards were also accompanied by a monetary reward: $2,000 for Wright and $1,000 for Dillard. This amount of money was transformative for them, and they both used it to purchase homes and land for their families.

The following year, in 1912, a writer from *National Geographic* climbed the mountain with John Alley, a local teen, so he could photograph Fool's Rock for his story. Familiar with the mountain, the foolhardy teen ventured to the precipice of Fool's Rock and sat with his feet dangling over its narrow edge—not even three feet wide—in the hopes of being photographed. The writer was so disturbed by the sight that he promised the boy five dollars, more than a week's wages in those days, to lure him back to safety.

Toward the end of your walk along the summit ridge, find the highest point on a rock, carved with, "Alt. 4,930 ft." You are now standing at the highest point of Whiteside Mountain, which is the central peak of the nearly four-mile-long massif, extending from Wildcat Gap to the base of Devil's Courthouse. The width, however, averages only about a half mile. After descending the last big slab of the pluton's summit at one and a half miles, you'll start a steep half-mile descent (**4**).

Pass by the final view at 1.6 miles, which looks west toward Highlands. Toward the bottom of the loop, steps have been installed to make the final stretch much easier. At 1.9 miles, the loop is complete, and you'll turn left to head 0.1 miles back to the parking lot.

CHEROKEE HISTORY OF WHITESIDE MOUNTAIN

Native Cherokee referred to Whiteside Mountain as Sanigilâ'gi, a name for which there is no known meaning. According to Cherokee legend, Spearfinger, known to the Cherokee as U'tulun'ta, was a powerful witch who made her home near Whiteside Mountain. She possessed impenetrable skin that was hard as a rock and had a claw-like finger she hid beneath her robe. Spearfinger had tremendous strength, which enabled her to carry enormous boulders and mold them into one another. It's said she built a large rock bridge in the air from the Hiwassee River in Georgia to Cashiers, North Carolina. Whiteside Mountain's cliffs were created when part of this bridge was sheared off by a lightning strike.

Spearfinger was also a shapeshifting witch, and she was known to lure children by taking on the appearance of someone they knew. Once a child was in her lap, she would spear them with her sharp finger and eat their livers. Some say the legend of Spearfinger was created as a cautionary tale to keep children from exploring beyond the boundaries set by their elders. As you stand atop Whiteside Mountain, it's easy to appreciate why the Cherokee may have told this tale.

SHADOW OF THE BEAR

On Highway 64, between Cashiers and Highlands, the Rhodes Big View Overlook tantalizes visitors with views of Whiteside Mountain. In late afternoon from mid-October through early November, however, this overlook becomes especially memorable when the "Shadow of the Bear," a naturally occurring phenomenon, appears amid the colorful fall foliage. The small shadow initially appears in the valley, and then it grows to eventually resemble a larger-than-life profile of a bear.

The overlook and land where the bear appear are protected in perpetuity, thanks to the generosity of the Raoul-Alstaetter-Rhodes family. The family lived in Highlands for more than a century and donated the parcel on October 20, 2006, to the Highlands-Cashiers Land Trust. The mission of the Highlands-Cashiers Land Trust is to "work to protect valuable natural resources for all generations," and the organization has been conserving "forests, wetlands, and vistas that are home to the greatest number of rare and endemic plants and animals in the Southern Appalachians" since 1909.

CONTINUING EDUCATION

Marett, Bill. *Courage at Fool's Rock: A True Tale of Incredible Heroism at Whiteside Mountain*. McDonald Letter Shop, 1980.

Mooney, James. *History, Myths, and Sacred Formulas of the Cherokees*. Bright Mountain Books, 1992.

Zahner, Robert. *The Mountain at the End of the Trail: A History of Whiteside Mountain*. Independently published, 2000.

23

YELLOW MOUNTAIN LOOKOUT TOWER

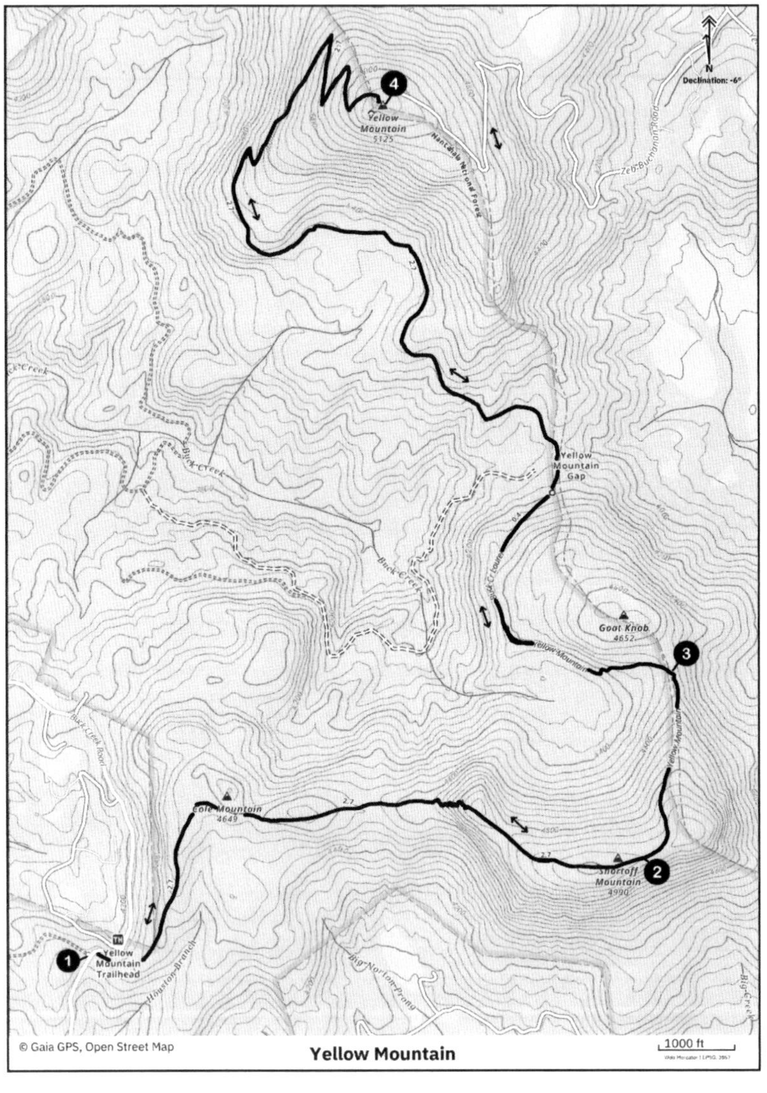

OVERVIEW

Cresting at 5,127 feet and straddling Jackson and Macon Counties, Yellow Mountain is the tallest peak in the Cowee Mountains. The well-weathered Yellow Mountain Lookout Tower awaits your visit at the craggy summit. The trail starts at a high elevation and never drops below 4,100 feet; however, there are numerous ascents and descents before the lookout tower that make the journey challenging, especially since you'll repeat them in the opposite direction on the second half of the hike. But the views that encompass four different states and nearly all of North Carolina's high mountain ranges are worth the sweat equity it takes to get there.

THE STATS

DISTANCE: 12.2 miles, round trip
DIFFICULTY: Most Difficult
ELEVATION GAIN AND LOSS: 2,497-foot gain, 2,497-foot loss
MAPS: USGS 7.5' Highlands; Glenville, National Geographic no. 229 Nantahala and Cullasaja Gorges
TRAILHEAD GPS: 35.10451, -83.20405
HIGHLIGHTS: Panoramic views, lookout tower, quiet forest
NOTES: Leashed dogs are allowed. There is limited parking at the trailhead.
DRIVING DIRECTIONS: From Highlands, at the intersection with NC-28, drive U.S. 64 (Cashiers Road) for 2.7 miles east to Buck Creek Road (State Road 1538). Turn left and drive 2.2 miles to Cody Gap. There are gravel pull-offs on both sides of the road, and the Yellow Mountain trailhead is on the right.

WAYPOINTS

1. Yellow Mountain Trailhead
2. side trail to the southern views (1.8 miles)
3. turn left at the signed junction (2.4 miles)
4. Yellow Mountain summit (5,127) and lookout tower (6.1 miles)

HIKE DESCRIPTION

The blue-blazed Yellow Mountain Trail begins at Cole Gap on the opposite side of the road from the parking area (**1**). The trail boasts a series of ascents, the first taking you nearly to the summit of Cole Mountain (4,649 feet). At 0.4 miles, a short side trail on the left leads to an overlook on the Western Cliffs.

After barely bypassing the summit of Cole Mountain, you'll continue through a broad saddle in a tranquil forest setting before beginning a second climb. At 1.3 miles, a series of short switchbacks ascends toward the summit of Shortoff Mountain. Just before the summit at 1.8 miles, there is a side trail on the right that leads to rocks slabs and views to the south (**2**).

Shortoff Mountain is the second-tallest peak in the Cowee Mountains (5,020 feet). On the summit, hikers are treated to a serene forest setting, with blankets of lush ferns and grasses lining the trail. The trail then dips and climbs on its course toward Goat Knob, the third peak along this roller coaster–style route.

At 2.4 miles, the trail turns left at a signed junction (**3**). After turning left, the trail drops, sometimes steeply, toward Yellow Mountain Gap. Pay careful attention as you approach this gap, as the trail has gone through reroutes and can be confusing. There is signage to help guide you.

At 3 miles, the trail crosses over a small spring. Soon after, an overgrown forest road leads in from the left, but continue straight on the worn trail. The trail leaves the forest road at 3.5 miles, turning right at the junction and arriving at Yellow Mountain Gap in another 0.1 miles. At the gap, you'll veer left at the next junction.

From Yellow Mountain Gap, the lowest point on the hike, you'll embark on your final ascent up the western side of Yellow Mountain, gaining nearly two thousand feet over the next three miles. You'll know you're nearing the summit when you reach a series of increasingly shorter switchbacks. After six miles, the trail reaches another T-junction, but continue to the right. You'll soon reach another similar junction where you'll turn right again.

Your hard work will pay off when you reach Yellow Mountain Lookout Tower (**4**). From the enormous slab of rock at its base, enjoy views of Panthertown Valley to the east, Shortoff Mountain to the south (which you climbed) and Whiteside Mountain's broad ridge to the southeast. The body of water beyond Whiteside Mountain is Lake Jocassee. To the north, Kuwohi (formerly Clingmans Dome) and Mount LeConte in Great Smoky Mountains National Park are visible. The highest peaks of the Plott Balsam

Yellow Mountain Lookout Tower. *Photograph by the author.*

range can also be seen, including Waterrock Knob, Mount Lyn Lowry and Plott Balsam (chapter 17 hike).

Be sure to explore the lookout tower as well. There are ladder steps that lead to the catwalk surrounding the cab from the seven-and-a-half-foot-tall stone foundation. The structure was built in 1934 by Franklin Roosevelt's Depression-era Civilian Conservation Corps and was used for more than three decades to monitor the eastern half of the Nantahala National Forest until it was decommissioned in 1969. Initially, caretakers had to reach it on foot from a trail near Buck Creek. In the late 1960s, life got easier for them when a jeep road was built to reach the summit.

The tower stood in disrepair until the early 1990s, when Ron Carnes, a U.S. Forest Service staff member, led the charge to restore it. First, funds had to be raised. The local community pitched in and held a fundraiser foot race to the tower on the old jeep road leading to it. In 1992, funding was secured, and materials were brought in by helicopter for volunteer groups providing labor hours.

By 2009, the tower was once again in need of freshening up. This time, it was restored under the American Recovery and Reinvestment Act along with seven other fire towers in the region that needed work.

When you've had your fill of the area's natural and historic beauty, retrace your route back to Cole Gap.

PART IV

DUPONT STATE RECREATIONAL FOREST

24

CEDAR ROCK AND BRIDAL VEIL FALLS

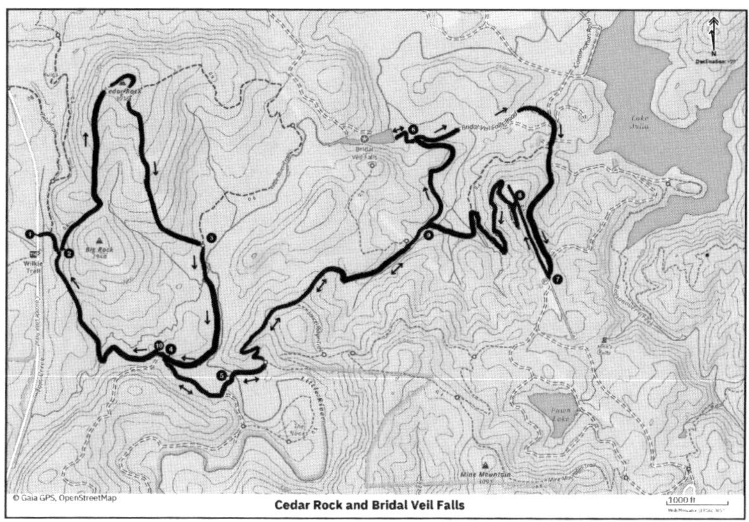

Cedar Rock and Bridal Veil Falls

OVERVIEW

Dupont State Recreational Forest's waterfalls have achieved legendary status over the years, providing the backdrop for scenes in blockbuster movies like *The Hunger Games.* This hike, however, avoids the crowds of the popular "waterfall loop" hike (chapter 25), but it's hardly a compromise. On this hike, you'll stand at the base of Bridal Veil Falls, which make an appearance in *The Last of the Mohicans*.

Waterfalls aren't the only highlight of the journey though. You'll walk across the broad granite summit of Cedar Rock and traverse an old airstrip that plays a lesser-known role in *The Hunger Games*. The Airstrip Trail dead ends at one of the most scenic vistas in the entire 12,500-plus acres of this recreational state forest, the only one of its kind in North Carolina.

THE STATS

Distance: 8.7 miles, lollipop loop
Difficulty: Moderate
Elevation Gain and Loss: 1,004-foot gain, 1,016-foot loss
Maps: USGS 7.5' Standingstone Mountain; National Geographic no. 504 Dupont State Recreational Forest, Dupont State Recreational Forest
Trailhead GPS Coordinates: 35.17284, -82.63899
Highlights: Famous waterfall, granite-topped Cedar Rock
Notes: Due to the unbridged water crossing at Corn Mill Shoals, do not attempt this hike after heavy or prolonged rain. Hiking poles are recommended for the crossing, as the stone slabs are very slick. Leashed dogs are allowed. This is a family-friendly hike, and portable toilets are available at the trailhead.
Driving Directions: North of Brevard, from Pisgah Forest at the intersection of NC-280 and U.S. 276, take U.S. 64 east for 3.7 miles to the traffic light at Crab Creek Road. Turn right on Crab Creek Road and follow it for 4.2 miles. Turn right on Dupont Road and follow it for a total of 4 miles (it will become Staton Road) to its end at Cascade Lock Road. Turn left on Cascade Lock Road, and in 0.6 miles, turn left into the Corn Mill Shoals Trailhead.

WAYPOINTS

1. trailhead
2. turn left on Big Rock Trail (0.1 miles)
3. turn right on Little River Trail (2.3 miles)
4. bear left on Corn Mill Shoals Trail (2.0 miles)
5. Little River crossing (2.4 miles)
6. stay left on Bridal Veil Falls Road (3.9 miles)
7. turn right onto the airstrip (5.1 miles)
8. turn right on Airstrip Trail (5.5 miles)
9. turn left on Shelter Rock Trail (6.5 miles)
10. veer left to stay on Corn Mill Shoals Trail (7.9 miles)

HIKE DESCRIPTION

Cross Cascade Lake Road at the trailhead and start your journey on the other side of the metal pole gate on Corn Mills Shoals Road, staying right where the Longside Trail veers left (**1**). Turn left on Big Rock Trail at 0.1 miles and ascend through its scattered namesake rocks (**2**). In just under 0.5 miles, enjoy the intermittent views of the Blue Ridge from the trail and adjacent stone slabs. At 0.8 miles, you'll crest the hill before ducking back into the woods and beginning a gentle descent on more dirt and rock among a multitude of pines.

Just before the one-mile mark, you'll summit Cedar Rock. Look for a narrow slab path between the pines leading to a wooden trail sign that indicates the junction of Big Rock and Cedar Rock Trail. Take Cedar Rock Trail to the right and begin descending to the south on pitted slab among a sea of lichen and moss islands.

At 1.5 miles, you'll turn right onto the Little River Trail, which runs alongside its namesake river (**3**). The forest is so thick with dog hobble, mountain laurel and rhododendron that you'll likely only hear the river rather than see it. Then you'll rock hop across Tom Creek and bear left onto the Corn Mill Shoals Trail (**4**). You'll continue down this trail past the Burnt Mountain Trail intersection and, at 2.4 miles, arrive at the unbridged crossing of Little River (**5**). If the water is high from recent rains, do not attempt this crossing and turn back. If the water appears safe and does not rise above your knees, cross slowly because the slab you'll traverse is slick. The best place to cross is slightly upstream from the trail to the right of the large dead pine on the bank.

Once you're across the creek, you'll stay left with the Corn Mill Shoals Trail and travel through a fern glade before you ascend a series of switchbacks. At 2.9 miles, Little River Trail veers to the right, but you'll stay straight and head downhill. You'll bisect a power line clearing at mile 3.4 and stay straight at the signed Bridal Overlook Trail. This out-and-back trail will add an additional mile to your day, if you'd like to tack it on.

Shelter Rock Trail veers right 0.1 miles beyond the Bridal Overlook Trail junction, but you'll stay left on Corn Mill Shoals Trail. Just before the 4-mile mark, you'll start hearing the falls and arrive at the junction with Bridal Veil Falls Road. Then you'll turn left and, in another 0.1 miles, pass a viewing deck with the enormity of the 120-foot-tall cascade spread before you. Beyond the deck, you'll arrive at the base of the falls, where rock slabs invite you to sit and stay a while. These falls appear in the 1992 film *The Last of the Mohicans* when a group finds the falls and hides behind

them in caves. However, the caves do not exist at the falls; they were part of the movie set.

You'll backtrack to Bridal Veil Falls Road and follow it instead of turning back onto Corn Mill Shoals Trail (**6**). Shortly after you pass a barn, picnic tables and a fire pit will appear on the right. Then you'll turn right on gravel Conservation Road, head uphill and pass Shelter Rock Trail on the right and Lake Julia Trail on the left.

At 5.1 miles, Summit Road feeds in from the right, but you'll continue straight and toward the fenced metal building with a sign that reads, "Summit elevation 2800." Take a right onto the Airstrip Trail, which is indeed an old airstrip, now used only by outdoor enthusiasts who wish to enjoy the state forest unless a nearby plane needs a place to land in an emergency (**7**).

The airstrip was built by Ben Cart, who started Summit Camps, traditional boys and girls summer camps, on forty acres he purchased from DuPont Corporation in 1967. The camps operated from 1969 to 1985, and Cart built the airstrip for his personal use in 1979. This aviation enthusiast flew many types of planes, but the Focke-Wulf single-seater German plane he owned was his favorite.

When the camps closed, Cart sold the land to Dupont Corporation, which used the airstrip to fly its executives to and from the property. In more recent

Opposite: Cedar Mountain summit. *Photograph by the author.*

Above: Base of Bridal Veil Falls. *Beverly MacDowell.*

Airstrip Trail. *Photo by the author.*

history, the Airstrip Trail was filmed from a helicopter with a wide-angle lens affixed to it, to capture the airstrip and the forest on either side of it. With the aid of computer-generated imagery, a train was superimposed on this footage to create the scene in *The Hunger Games* in which Katniss and Peeta are traveling through District 12 to the Capitol.

Follow the airstrip all the way to its end to enjoy the magnificent view of Pisgah National Forest. On a clear day, you can spot the transmission tower on Mount Pisgah's summit (chapter 10 hike). Turn around and look for the signed Airstrip Trail that continues into the woods to the right (**8**). You'll descend on the trail using switchbacks for nearly a mile until you reach the junction with Shelter Rock Trail, where you'll turn left (**9**).

In another 0.2 miles, you'll turn left onto Corn Mill Shoals Trail. If the area looks familiar, this is because it's the trail you hiked to the falls earlier. For the next half mile, the trail climbs, passing Laurel Ridge Trail on the left, before it drops down to the Corn Mill Shoals water crossing, which you'll ford a second time.

You'll continue on Corn Mill Shoals Trail, veering left to continue on it at 7.9 miles (**10**) until it ends at the Cascade Lake Road and the trailhead, passing by the Little River, Burnt Mountain Trail, Shoals Trail and Big Rock Trail junctions along the way.

DUPONT FOREST: A WIN FOR CONSERVATION

At first glance, DuPont may seem an unusual name for a state forest if you're familiar with the American chemical company with the same name. Before 1996, DuPont ran a plant on the property; however, in 1995, local environmental groups had great interest in facilitating discussions between three entities—DuPont, the State of North Carolina and The Conservation Fund, a national nonprofit organization whose mission is dedicated to "the business of conservation"—when DuPont expressed interest in selling its property and plant separately.

As a result of this activism, DuPont sold 7,600 acres to the State of North Carolina in 1997, hence creating DuPont State Recreational Forest. Funding for the $2.2 million bargain sale was possible thanks to the North Carolina Natural Heritage Trust Fund, a state trust organization dedicated to protecting game lands. About 1,750 acres of the property was registered with the North Carolina Heritage Program because they have important ecological significance. People began enjoying the new state forest that was created from the sale immediately, especially marveling at the beauty of Hooker Falls, the only significant waterfall that was acquired through the purchase.

DuPont sold the surrounding 2,700 acres and the plant to Sterling Diagnostic Imaging, which used it to manufacture X-ray film. In 1999, Sterling listed 2,200 acres, including Triple Falls, High Falls and Bridal Veil Falls, for sale. The Conservation Fund once again stepped up to represent the State of North Carolina in acquiring this highly attractive land. Sterling was indifferent to the public's pleas to sell the land to the state and implemented a "private, secretive bidding process," according to the Friends of Dupont Forest's website. Although the Conservation Fund had bid $5.5 million for the land, developer Jim Anthony of the Cliffs Community acquired it for $6.35 million. Despite strong appeals from not only the public but also George Bush and Governor Jim Hunt, Sterling would not allow the state to match Anthony's bid.

Anthony initially expressed that he had no interest in developing the land and instead intended to use it as a private retreat. However, it was discovered that he had crafted a complex legal agreement with Sterling that allowed him to develop the land, despite the recorded land deed that stated it could not be used for residential development. By the end of 1999, Anthony had announced his plan to develop the property and filed plans with Transylvania County to build a massive gated residential community, with High Falls, Triple Falls and Bridal Veil Falls as the centerpiece. Chet Meinzer, the DuPont property manager, discouraged Anthony from proceeding, stating the X-ray film plant was still operational and that implementing his proposed development would potentially create a chemical environmental risk. Anthony was indifferent to his pleas, but the public outcry about this shady legal agreement was far from complacent.

A group of locals, including Jeff Jennings, a DuPont plant employee who was instrumental in the initial property sale to the state, banded together to form Friends of the Falls in April 2000. Intense activism ensued for the next six months, and it captured the attention of key power players in Raleigh. That it was an election year likely also helped draw necessary attention from these politicians. Whatever the motive, the work of those who fought to save the land and falls from environmental destruction and keep them accessible to the public paid off.

On October 23, 2000, Governor Jim Hunt and the North Carolina Council of State unanimously voted to invoke the power of eminent domain to the 2,223 acres of the property. The purchase price, $24 million, was far more expensive, over four times the price Anthony had paid. While developing the property for the residential community he had planned, Anthony had built a covered bridge at the top of High Falls as well as a second one at the outflow of Lake Julia. He had also built a road leading to Bridal Veil Falls, all of which he argued justified the higher price.

In a letter dated November 1, 2000, from Attorney General Mike Easley to those who had sent messages of support for protection of the property and falls, the following was conveyed:

> *The Council of State voted to acquire the forest property that had been slated for development. The action followed many long months of negotiations by my lawyers, who had the difficult task of fully exploring whether a voluntary agreement could ever be reached to achieve the State's goals of adequately protecting water quality and preserving the watershed*

> *and waterfalls for the people.... The State's only choice was to acquire the threatened property by the power of eminent domain and thus make the DuPont Forest whole.*

Of course, there are always two sides to a story, and this one is no exception. A contingency of citizens disagreed with the state's decision and believed the government had overstepped its bounds. Whichever side of the controversy you stand on, it would be a shame to miss experiencing this magical land of waterfalls.

CONTINUING EDUCATION

Bernstein, Danny. *DuPont Forest: A History*. The History Press, 2020.

25

WATERFALL LOOP

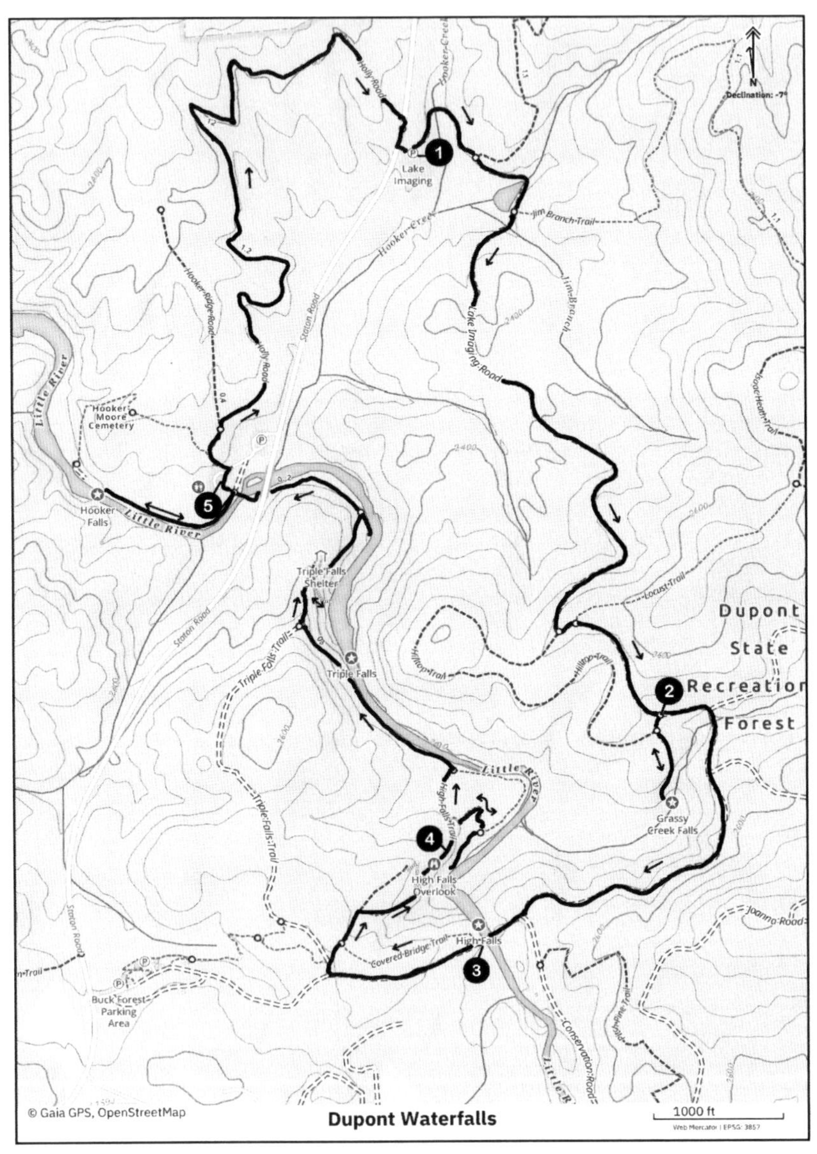

If waterfalls are your thing, then this is your hike. You'll visit four of the six major cataracts in this treasure of a preserve as you reflect on modern history. You'll also discover a lasting artifact of the controversy that allows you to visit two of these falls at all. This hike is also a movie lover's delight, as *The Hunger Games* and *The Last of the Mohicans* were both filmed along this route.

Consider yourself warned that this is a very popular hike and you will almost assuredly have company on it. Avoid weekends and try to arrive early in the morning or later in the afternoon if you prefer more solitude.

THE STATS

Distance: 6.4 miles
Difficulty: Moderate
Elevation Gain and Loss: 684-foot gain, 684-foot loss
Maps: USGS 7.5' Standingstone Mountain; National Geographic no. 504 Dupont State Recreational Forest, Dupont State Recreational Forest
Trailhead GPS Coordinates: 35.20930, -82.61558
Highlights: Four waterfalls, Lake Imaging
Notes: Leashed dogs are allowed. This is a family-friendly hike. There is a primitive toilet at the trailhead and restrooms available at the High Falls parking area, which you'll hike through. Mountain bikers and equestrians also use these trails, and both cyclists and hikers should yield to horses. Do not climb on or beside the falls and use caution if you swim near the base of any waterfall. DuPont's waterfalls have claimed lives.
Driving Directions: North of Brevard, from Pisgah Forest at the intersection of NC-280 and U.S. 276, take U.S. 64 east for 3.7 miles to the traffic light at Crab Creek Road. Turn right on Crab Creek Road and follow it 4.2 miles. Turn right on Dupont Road and follow it for 2.5 miles (it will become Staton Road) to the Lake Imaging Trailhead on your left.

WAYPOINTS

1. Lake Imaging Trailhead
2. turn right on Grassy Creek Trail (1.4 miles)
3. bridge over the top of Triple Falls (2.4 miles)
4. clearing with a view of Triple Falls (2.8 miles)
5. Hooker Falls parking area and restrooms (4.2 miles)

HIKE DESCRIPTION

From the parking area, you'll pass around the metal pole gate to start your hike on Lake Imaging Road (**1**). In less than a quarter mile, you'll arrive at Lake Imaging, one of the five lakes on the state forest property, whose name was given to it by Sterling Diagnostic Imaging, a former owner of this land. Only consuming two acres, it's more of a pond than a lake, but it's a lovely spot to take a photograph. You'll stay to the left on Lake Imaging Road and pass the Jim Branch Trail on the left before you ascend through mountain laurel and pine.

At the 0.8-mile mark, you'll cross through an area of pines that was once a clearing. At 1.2 miles, you'll cross over rock slabs before passing Hilltop Trail that comes in from the right followed by Locust Trail that veers left. At 1.4 miles, you'll turn right on Grassy Creek Trail and pass by the other end of Hilltop Trail (**2**). Grassy Creek Falls is just ahead after a short descent, where you'll stand alongside the 50-foot-tall sliding fall as it rushes down a lengthy granite slab. There are user trails that parallel the fall on its downward trajectory, but the vegetation is dense, and I don't recommend venturing far.

You'll backtrack to Lake Imaging Road and continue your journey to the right. At 1.8 miles, Buck Forest Road feeds in on the left, but you'll continue right to cross Grassy Creek on a bridge. Chestnut Oak Road leads to the left shortly after the bridge, but you'll continue straight on Buck Forest Road and travel up a hill before you pass Conservation Road at 2.4 miles.

Then you'll keep straight and walk across the picturesque covered bridge over Little River that was built by Jim Anthony, the developer who owned the land for a brief period before the State of North Carolina acquired it by eminent domain (see *Dupont: A Win for Conservation* in chapter 24). Take a moment to look at High Falls from the right side of the bridge. You're standing at the top of it, and its base is your next stop (**3**).

Then you'll veer right on the Covered Bridge Trail after the bridge and turn right again onto High Falls Trail. At 2.8 miles, there is a clearing to the right along a split-rail fence with a picture-perfect view of the falls (**4**).

Crashing 120 feet from the bridge you were standing on just minutes before, the falls are a sight to behold. Next, you'll take a right on River Bend Trail, which will bring you close to the river's edge to see the falls. Then you'll backtrack to High Falls Trail and turn right to walk alongside a much calmer portion of Little River.

At 3.8 miles, you'll turn right on the Triple Falls Trail and take the wooden steps on the right that descend to the middle tier of Triple Falls,

Triple Falls. *Melissa Gibson.*

which drops a collective 125 feet through its three stages. Head back up the steps and on Triple Falls Trail to the right where you'll continue to visualize its trio of cascades. Triple Falls had its first cinematic appearance in *The Last of the Mohicans* during the scene in which the English escape the French and climb the falls. They were later made popular again in *The Hunger Games* when Katniss, the story's protagonist, runs across the top of them. Before you get any ideas of re-creating the scene, remember that accidents on or near waterfalls are often deadly or life-altering. The magic of film editing makes it appear otherwise, but Jennifer Lawrence, the actress who portrays Katniss, was secured by a wire from above, and she had boards to run on below her feet.

At 4.2 miles, you'll pass under Staton Road and then across an iron bridge over Little River. You'll arrive at the enormous Hooker Falls parking area, where restrooms await you if you need one after hearing rushing water for so much of the hike (**5**).

From the parking area, you'll look for the Hooker Falls Trail and head 0.3 miles downstream. You'll parallel Little River before you arrive at its elongated, 15-foot-wide, curtain-style base. On a warm day, it's almost guaranteed you'll find sunbathers on the rocks and people swimming in the pool below the falls. Hooker Falls was also used in *The Last of the Mohicans* in

Hooker Falls. *Photograph by the author.*

the scene where canoes plunge over the edge of a waterfall. It was named for the Hooker family who owned the property and ran a gristmill on it for more than thirty years.

Then you'll backtrack to the Hooker Falls parking area and look for Holly Road across the lot and behind a metal pole gate. You'll stay right as you pass a road that leads to the left to the Moore/Hooker Cemetery (private) as you traverse through pine-filled woods, likely with far less company than you previously had.

At 6.2 miles, you'll arrive at Staton Road and turn right to enter the Lake Imagine parking area, where you left your car at the hike's start.

CONTINUING EDUCATION

Mann, Michael, dir. *The Last of the Mohicans*. Michael Mann, 1992.

Ross, Gary, dir. *The Hunger Games*. Lions Gate, 2012.

PART V

CONSERVING CAROLINA TRAILS

26

HICKORY NUT GORGE

BEARWALLOW MOUNTAIN AND WILDCAT ROCK

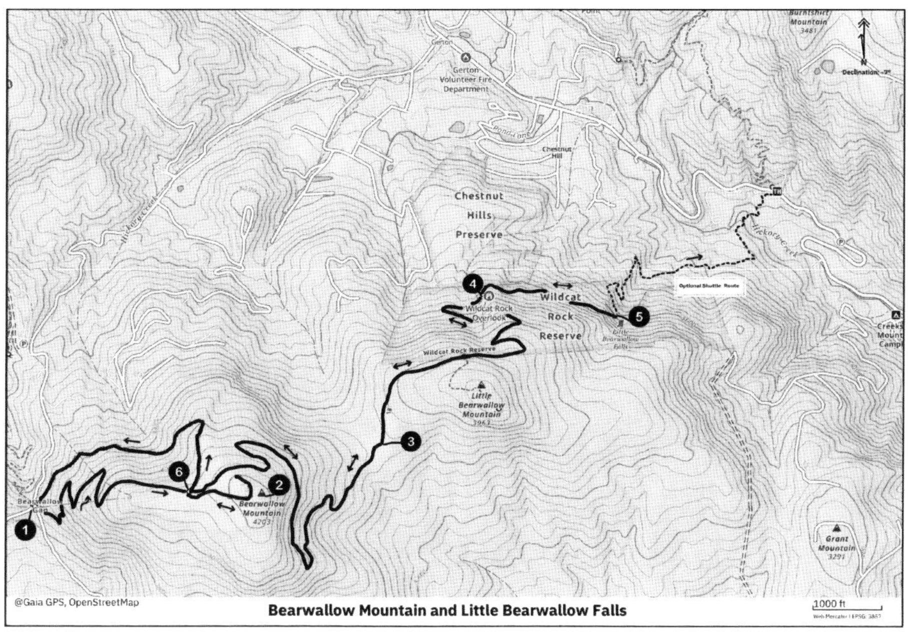

Bearwallow Mountain and Little Bearwallow Falls

OVERVIEW

Hickory Nut Gorge's fourteen-mile-long canyon cuts a rugged path through the Blue Ridge escarpment, creating a link between the Piedmont and the mountains. The first known paths through the gorge were created by the Cherokee, but you can thank Conserving Carolina, a land trust organization, for the trails you'll be hiking on this route. To date, they have saved over forty-eight thousand acres and created thirty-eight miles of trail.

This hike traverses through a landscape full of beautiful scenery to keep you entertained and challenged, including bucolic meadows, a colorful fire tower, rocky woods that lead to an even higher rocky perch with views into Hickory Nut Gap and a waterfall that is frequented by climbers.

In late 2020, Carolina Conservation added a 2-mile trail link between Bearwallow Mountain and Little Bearwallow Mountain. Both trails will eventually be part of a planned, connected 130-mile Hickory Nut Gorge State Trail System. The nearby Florence Nature Preserve and Trombatore Trail, also part of Conservation Carolina's good work, are included in this plan, and both are worthy of exploration as well.

THE STATS

Distance: 7.9 miles, out and back (or 6 miles for the one-way shuttle hike)
Difficulty: Difficult
Elevation Gain and Loss: 1,769-foot gain, 1,769-foot loss (This is true if the hike is completed as the out-and-back option. There is considerably less climbing if the hike is completed as a one-way shuttle hike from Bearwallow to Wildcat Rock.)
Maps: Conserving Carolina website map; USGS 7.5' Bat Cave
Trailhead GPS Coordinates: 35.46069, -82.36787
Highlights: Bearwallow Mountain summit views and fire tower, Little Bearwallow meadow, Wildcat Rock, Little Bearwallow Falls
Notes: Leashed dogs are allowed. The trails are open from dawn to dusk, no camping allowed.
Driving Directions: From downtown Asheville, take I-240 east to exit 9, Blue Ridge Parkway/Bat Cave, to join U.S. 74A. Take U.S. 74A east for 12.7 miles and then turn right on Bearwallow Mountain Road. Follow it for 2.1 miles to Bearwallow Gap. There are parking spaces on either side of the road.

WAYPOINTS

1. Bearwallow Mountain Trailhead
2. Bearwallow Mountain summit (0.8 mile)
3. Little Bearwallow meadow (2.4 miles)
4. Wildcat Rock overlook spur trail (3.6 miles)
5. Little Bearwallow Falls (mile 4.0)
6. intersection with fire tower access road (7 miles)

DESCRIPTION

Bearwallow Mountain Trail starts on the east side of Bearwallow Gap, just beyond the wooden arbor trail sign (**1**). Take note of the gravel fire tower access road to the left of the trail—you'll have the option to descend it at the end of this hike. Bearwallow Mountain Trail was constructed in 2011, after Conservation Carolina secured an eighty-one-acre easement in 2009. For years, people accessed the summit via the fire tower road; now, a well-constructed trail leads the way.

Almost immediately, the trail begins to climb on switchbacks with thoughtfully placed stairs. In 0.7 miles, you'll climb a flight of stone steps with large boulders nearby. In the winter, the steps are often covered in ice, so be mindful of your step. Bearwallow Mountain's extensive bald and panoramic views will greet you soon after you ascend the last step (**2**). To the west are the Great Balsams and their highest peak, Mount Pisgah (chapter 10). Hickory Nut Gorge sits below you in the east; the Black Mountains, including Mount Mitchell, are to the north (chapter 16); and Hendersonville and then South Carolina are to the south.

Bearwallow Mountain got its name from the small wetland located in the saddle between Bearwallow and Little Bearwallow Mountain. According to Conserving Carolina trail specialist Peter Barr, "Here, water rises from the ground and pools on the ridegeline of the mountain…historically it has been the location where bears go to 'wallow,' cooling off in the wet mud."

It's hard to miss the forty-seven-foot-tall fire tower with its mustard yellow cab and hodgepodge of other antennae nearby. The steel tower was built in 1934 by the Civilian Conservation Corps and decommissioned in 1994. A firewatcher resided on the bald and kept watch for smoke in the valleys of Rutherford, Buncombe and Henderson Counties.

Once you've taken in your fill of the sweeping summit views and walked to the base of the fenced fire tower, you'll walk toward the rest of the antennae on the faint gravel road until you reach its end. Downhill from this spot, you'll turn right onto Wildcat Rock Trail, which cuts through the meadow. There's a green trail sign that marks its location on the edge of the meadow before it ducks into the woods around 1.3 miles.

Look for the well-placed round, orange Conserving Carolina trail markers on trees to keep you on track. For the next two miles, you will walk on the trail that was added in 2020. It passes between large swaths of rhododendron and gently rolls along for nearly half a mile. When it begins to descend in earnest, look to your left to spot an opening where you can see Chimney

Rock Mountain rising sharply from the gorge's valley floor along with Rich Mountain and then Sugarloaf standing tall to the right. You'll also catch a glimpse of Lake Lure's western inlet, where the Broad River spills into it.

At 1.9 miles, the trail makes a sharply angled left turn as it descends. In another 0.5 miles, the trail reaches a saddle below Little Bearwallow's summit (**3**). Chimney Rock Mountain, Rich Mountain and Sugarloaf are easier to spot in this grassy highland. A stately tulip tree stands beside the trail in the meadow. You'll continue past it and head back into the woods on the other side of the meadow. Just before you enter the woods, turn around. You'll be treated to a close-range view of Bearwallow Mountain with a couple of antennae peeking out.

This section of Wildcat Rock Trail was opened in 2017. It even won the Coalition of Recreational Trails National Award for trail design and construction, thanks to the hard work of its designer, Peter Barr. The terrain is less forgiving though, so take it slow on the rocky terrain and appreciate the hard work that went into creating this footpath. After you pass by some impressive rock faces and cliffs, you'll arrive at the turnoff to Wildcat Rock Overlook on the right at mile 3.6 (**4**).

The short but steep side trail will lead you up over ninety well-placed stone steps through a labyrinth of enormous boulders. Signs mark the way to the top, where you will be treated to views of Little Pisgah Mountain to the north, Blue Ridge Pastures to the west and Hickory Nut Gap to the northwest. It's a fantastic spot to rest before you continue.

Backtrack to the main trail and take a right to head toward Little Bearwallow Falls, which you'll arrive at around the four-mile mark (**5**). The one-hundred-foot-tall waterfall slides down a broad cliff and is frequented by rock climbers year round. Don't expect to hear the falls before you see them though—they're not raging torrents at any time and all but thin ribbons most days (sometimes they're even dried up completely). The enormity of the rock face is my favorite part of the entire scene.

Retrace your steps, passing the spur trail to the Wildcat Rock overlook, until you reach Bearwallow's summit at mile 6.9. Then you'll pass over the bald on the trail until it bisects a gravel road. This is the other end of the fire tower access road you encountered at the start of the hike (**6**). You can either descend Bearwallow Mountain Trail back to the trailhead or take the gravel road for a change of scenery.

If you are inspired by this hike, check out Conserving Carolina's website (www.conservingcarolina.org) to learn more about their work and how you can help them continue their mission to "protect, restore, and inspire appreciation of the natural world."

Saddle Meadow below Little Bearwallow Mountain. *Photograph by the author.*

The author admiring the view at Wildcat Rock. *Photograph by the author.*

BEARWALLOW AND THE STORM OF THE CENTURY

In the early 1990s, Judy Tuten was the Bearwallow Mountain Lookout Tower's operator, and she lived on the mountain with her husband and son.

In the winter of 1993, what would be dubbed the "storm of the century" descended on the region, dumping two feet of snow in blizzard conditions. The winds were so strong during the storm that Tuten was scared the house would be uprooted, as the soil on the bald is only a couple of inches deep.

She and her family survived the ordeal and were shocked to see the bald summit mostly free of snow when they walked outside after the storm passed two days later. That snow had to go somewhere though. Imagine the family's surprise to find it banked right up against their home and burying their cars in an eleven-foot tall, two-hundred-foot-long drift—compliments of the storm's raging winds.

Bearwallow Mountain is part of the Blue Ridge escarpment and the Blue Ridge Mountain Range, rising sharply from the Piedmont. The topography of this escarpment creates a unique situation when storms approach from the Gulf of Mexico. Oftentimes, they will slow down over the area and release the bulk of their precipitation; this also creates much stronger winds on mountain summits. Tuten and her family certainly witnessed this phenomenon, and she later admitted it was one of her favorite memories of her six-year tenure on the mountain.

THE LEGEND OF THE HICKORY NUT GORGE LITTLE PEOPLE

One of the most interesting stories about Hickory Nut Gorge involves the legend of the "Little People," spirits known as Yunwi Tsundsdi to the Cherokee, who lived in rock caves throughout the gorge. Their hair was so long it nearly touched the earth, yet their bodies barely reached up to a man's knee. Much of their time was spent dancing and drumming, and they loved music.

The Little People were known to be charitable and helpful and even led lost children back to their parents. But if someone discovered the Little People's habitat, they would have a spell cast on them that would cause them to wander in a permanent daze. The Little People's home in Hickory Nut Gorge was sacred to them, and they guarded the gorge's entrances closely. Those who tried to pass through often disappeared.

The Cherokee had been gifted a form of wild tobacco that grew just outside the gorge near "the big waters." They smoked the tobacco, but they also used it for medicinal purposes and in rituals as a means to drive away evil spirits. To obtain more of the prized plant, they had to pass through the gorge, which all but guaranteed interactions with the Little People. During a Cherokee council meeting, a young warrior volunteered to make the journey, confident he would return safely.

He never returned, and the next to step up for the perilous task was a magician who could disguise himself. He posed as a mole first, but he narrowly escaped the Little People after he was caught burrowing through the gorge. Next, he transformed himself into a hummingbird, but he was only able to bring a small supply of tobacco back to his people. For his third attempt, he turned himself into a whirlwind. As he spun wildly through the gorge, trees were stripped from the landscape, and exposed rock cliffs took their place. The force of his power also scattered enormous boulders into nearby rivers and streams. Evidence of the destruction he left in his wake is still evident.

The whirlwind's power was so intense that the Little People fled, and the magician found the bones of the warrior who had previously disappeared in a riverbed. He revived the man's remains and returned home with a bounty of tobacco for their people.

SHUTTLE OPTION

This hike can be completed as a one-way, six-mile shuttle hike that is easier than the described out-and-back option. If you choose this option, I recommend starting on the Bearwallow Mountain Trail side, since there is significantly less climbing from this direction. Coordinates for the second trailhead are 35.47329, -82.33202, which is located on Highway 74A in Gerton, across the street from the Florence Nature Preserve.

CONTINUING EDUCATION

Lossiah, Lynn. *Secrets and Mysteries of the Cherokee Little People*. Cherokee Publications, 1998.

27

BRACKEN PRESERVE

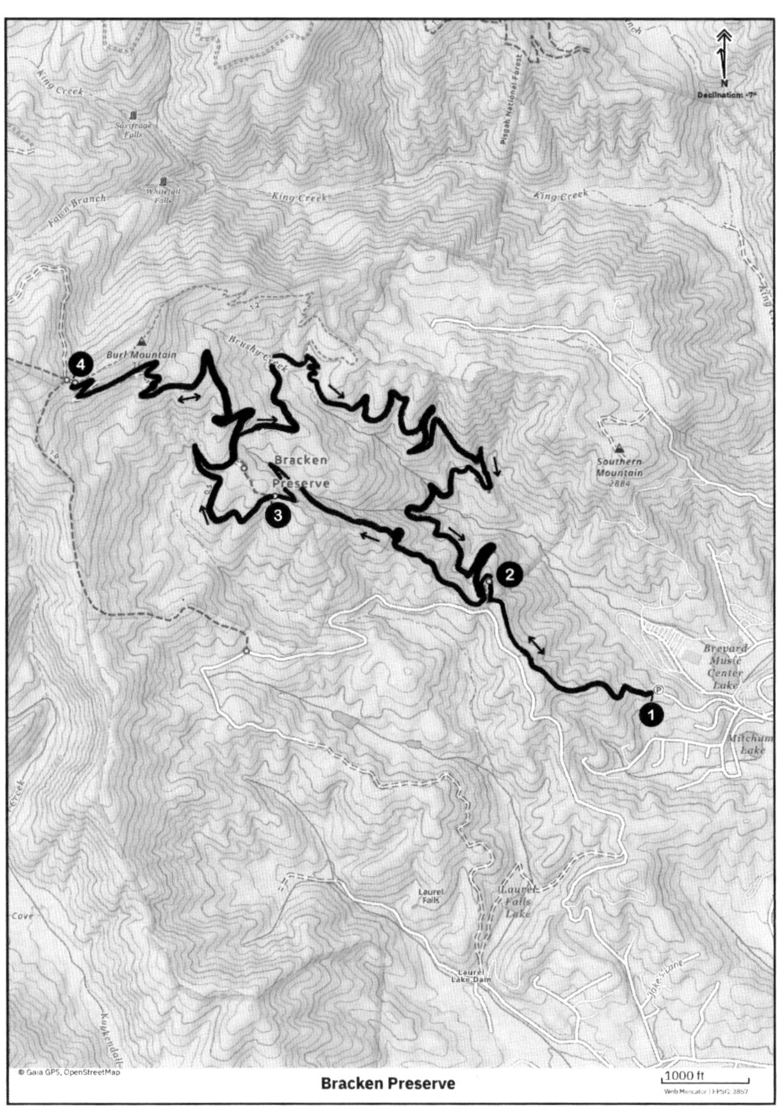

Bracken Preserve was the City of Brevard's first municipal water supply source, and the land, totaling 395 acres, was purchased in the early 1900s. Nowadays, outdoor enthusiasts can enjoy the beauty of this special preserve that borders Pisgah National Forest, since its days as a water supply are long over. With over nine miles of trail in the preserve and ongoing efforts to create more, it's easy to spend an entire day enjoying this exemplar of conservation just minutes from downtown Brevard. Educational signs peppered throughout the preserve's trail network are a nice perk and treat visitors to the human and natural history of this protected land.

THE STATS

Distance: 8 miles
Difficulty: Difficult
Elevation Gain and Loss: 1,138-foot gain, 1,123-foot loss
Maps: Conserving Carolina website (www.conservingcarolina.org); The trailhead map may be outdated, but there is a QR code on it to download the most current map of the preserve.
Trailhead GPS Coordinates: 35.24087, -82.75596
Highlights: Interpretive signage with natural and human history, fall foliage, small water features, biodiverse coves
Notes: Leashed dogs are allowed. Trails are open to mountain bikers.
Driving Directions: From downtown Brevard, head west on Main Street. Turn right on Galloway Street and then left on Probart Street. Follow Probart Street for 0.6 miles, and then turn right on Music Camp Road. After 0.3 miles, veer left onto gravel Pinnacle Road. Follow Pinnacle Road for 0.2 miles until it dead ends at the Bracken Preserve parking area.

WAYPOINTS

1. Bracken Mountain Trailhead
2. Brushy Creek Trail intersection (0.6 miles)
3. Mackey Ridge Trail intersection (1.9 miles)
4. Pisgah National Forest boundary and Pinnacle Trail (3.1 miles)

DESCRIPTION

Blue-blazed Bracken Mountain Trail ascends immediately from the parking area, passing a couple of picnic tables within a few steps (**1**). After climbing a few short switchbacks to avoid crossing onto private property, the grade lessens as the preserve property becomes less encumbered.

At 0.6 miles, Brushy Creek Trail appears on the right, and there is an informational sign highlighting the cultural history of the area (**2**). You'll continue left to stay on Bracken Mountain Trail. Mountain laurel and rhododendron dominate the landscape as you climb, thanks to the acidic, nutrient-poor soil of this pine-oak-heath forest.

After passing a couple more informational signs, you'll reach a forked intersection at the one-and-a-half-mile mark. Mackey Ridge Trail heads uphill to the right, but you'll stay left. As you climb, look for a patch of a low-lying evergreen plants that resemble miniature cedar trees or a mop of hair on a Dr. Seuss storybook character. Despite this plant's quirky appearance and its common names of running or ground cedar, it's not even remotely related to cedar. It's a clubmoss; however, this name is also misleading, since it's not classified as moss either. These primitive vascular plants are more closely related to ferns, and their spores were once used to create lycopodium powder for flash photography.

Just under 2 miles, Mackey Ridge Trail appears on the right, but you'll continue straight (**3**). At 3.1 miles, you'll reach the junction with Pisgah National Forest at a T-intersection in the trail (**4**). The Pinnacle Trail heads off to the right. The trail was named for the former Pinnacle community who lived in the area. Two of its founders, Laughing Water, a woman from the Blackfoot Nation, and Tom, a Black man, both escaped captivity and came to the area in 1860 to avoid contracting typhoid fever.

You'll retrace your footsteps down Bracken Mountain Trail for a mile until you reach the intersection with Mackey Ridge Trail (yellow blaze), which you passed earlier, and turn left onto it. This short trail, named for a family who once settled in this area, divides the eastern and western sections of the preserve, as well as the Bracken Creek and Brushy Creek watersheds.

In less than 200 feet, you'll arrive at another intersection. Mackey Ridge Trail continues to the right for 0.2 miles to its lower junction with Bracken Mountain Trail. Red-blazed Brushy Mountain Trail is to the left, and that's the direction you'll head.

Just under five miles in, a short trail to the right leads to a shelter that was built by a local Boy Scouts of America troop. Continuing, you'll pass the

Running cedar in Bracken Preserve. *Photograph by the author.*

lower junction with the Pinnacle Trail on the left, several more informational signs and a series of three bridges beside small cascades.

The third cascade at 6.6 miles, Renzulli Falls, is named for Carlo Renzulli, an Italian-born professional violinist whose family supported the Brevard Music Center and whose generosity helped make public access to the preserve possible with a right of way. The music center's campus sits below and downstream from this crossing.

At 7.2 miles, you'll arrive at the junction with Bracken Mountain Trail. Then you'll turn left and follow it for 0.6 miles to the parking area.

SAVING BRACKEN PRESERVE

By the late 1980s, Cathey's Creek had been the source of Brevard's municipal water for nearly a decade; however, the city still owned nearly four hundred acres it had purchased in the early 1900s for this purpose. It implemented an appraisal and timber study to assess the viability of developing or selling the property. Another decade passed, and the fate of the land sat in limbo until the early 2000s, when the town was facing financial woes.

Mayor Jimmy Harris and local resident Mac Morrow took a walk on the property after a troubling council meeting in which the idea of selling the land to a local developer was brought up. By the end of their jaunt through the pristine woods, the mayor decided that preserving the land for public enjoyment was a far more valuable long-term goal than selling it for development. For the next four years, Harris and Morrow worked to garner public support for their vision of preservation.

In 2004, the Brevard City Council voted to preserve the property and provide access to the public for low-impact recreational activities. One year later, the city received a $1.04 million grant from the North Carolina Clean Water Management Trust Fund to establish a permanent conservation easement on the property, which took effect in January 2007.

In January 2012, after crucial rights-of-way were obtained from property owners along Pinnacle Drive, the road that leads to the preserve's trailhead, work began to develop the first phase of the trails in Bracken. Since then, the trail network has grown, including the Pinnacle Trail, which links Bracken to Pisgah National Forest. In 2022, Conserving Carolina began working with the City of Brevard to raise the funds to bring thirty-four more acres into the fold.

PART VI

NATIONAL HISTORIC SITES

28

CARL SANDBURG HOME NATIONAL HISTORIC SITE

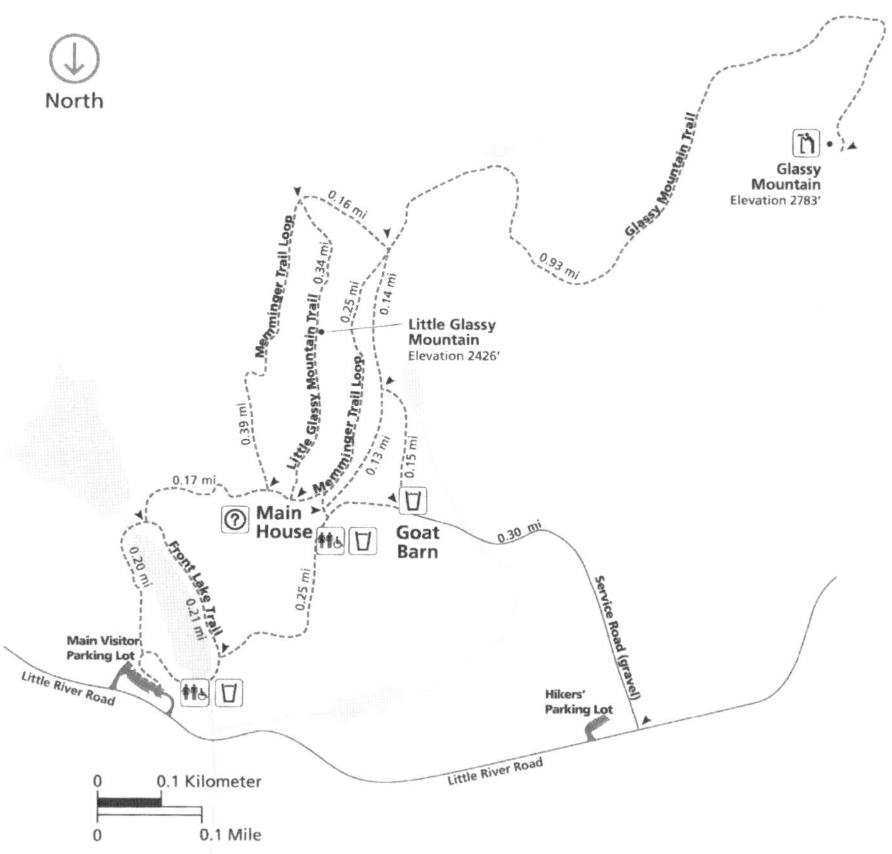

Carl Sandburg National Historic Site map. *National Park Service.*

OVERVIEW

Carl Sandburg, a first-generation American and Pulitzer Prize–winning writer, wore many hats throughout his life. He was a poet, journalist and biographer, but he was also a devoted family man with broad-ranging interests. Upon his retirement, in 1945, Sandburg retreated from Michigan to the mountains of Western North Carolina.

The family found the perfect home for his wife Lilian Sandburg's prize-winning dairy goats when they purchased Connemara, a 245-acre oasis just outside of Flat Rock. They resided in the home for nearly twenty-four years until the "poet of the people" died in 1967. The property was sold to the National Park Service (NPS) a year after his death.

I devoted this chapter as an itinerary of my favorite activities on the property, which include hiking to the Glassy Mountain overlook. It's a wonderful family destination, especially if you have animal-loving children, since descendants of Mrs. Sandburg's goats still live at Connemara, and the public is invited to interact with them.

THE STATS

Distance, Difficulty and Elevation Gain/Loss: varies, depending on your itinerary (the trails are easy to moderate)
Maps: Carl Sandburg Home NHS Trails map on site (free)
Trailhead GPS Coordinates: 35.27336, -82.44465
Highlights: Carl Sandburg home, goat farm, views from Glassy Mountain overlook
Notes: Leashed dogs are allowed. Restrooms are located on site. Grounds, trails and parking areas are open from sunrise to sunset, but no camping is allowed. Tours of the home can be reserved at www.recreation.gov (or you can call 828-693-4178 if the booking window is already closed on the day of your visit). A calendar of the site's special events can be found at www.nps.gov/carl.
Driving Directions: From the I-26 Upward Road Interchange (exit 53), turn right if exiting from I-26 East or left if exiting from I-26 West. Go 1.3 miles to the intersection with U.S. 176 and continue straight; the road turns into North Highland Lake Road. Continue 1.1 miles to NC-225 and turn left. Go 0.8 miles and turn right onto Little River Road (follow the signs). The parking area is on the left after 0.2 miles.

HIKE DESCRIPTION AND RECOMMENDATIONS

If you didn't reserve a spot for a docent-led tour of the Sandburg home online before you arrived, take care of that first since you can't tour the home without it. It will familiarize you with the close-knit Sandburg family and the writer's tremendous lifetime achievements. Bibliophiles will appreciate Sandburg's collection of over fourteen thousand books, which artfully line the shelves on the walls. The home feels as if the family has just stepped out for a hike on the tranquil property, and that's exactly the intent. The home's contents were donated after the NPS bought the property, and much of it was left as it was found.

Originally known as Rock Hill from 1838 to 1900, the property had a less than illustrious start. In 1838, the house that eventually became the Sandburgs' was partially built by enslaved laborers for an enslaver who served in the Confederate government. The following two owners fought to maintain racial segregation after Reconstruction. This was in stark contrast to Sandburg's views, as he received a lifetime membership to the National Association for the Advancement of Colored People (NAACP) for his efforts

Glassy Mountain overlook view. *Photograph by the author.*

to promote civil rights. Much of his Pulitzer Prize–winning work, *Complete Poems*, touches on social justice and labor rights.

Be sure to add a hike to the Glassy Mountain Overlook (2,782 feet) to your itinerary. There are several trails that lead to the summit, but my favorite route takes the western side of the Memminger Loop Trail and connects it with the Glassy Mountain Trail to the overlook.

While descending the mountain, you can either follow the east side of the Memminger Loop or follow the Little Glassy Trail, which cuts over the mountain between the Memminger Loop Trails (my preference). Look for a wooden chair behind the Sandburg home resting on a shaded rock slab. This was a familiar spot to Sandburg, who often retreated to it for reflection and to write. At the Glassy Mountain Overlook, benches placed by the NPS await visitors. In either of these spots, you'll likely agree with Sandburg, who once wrote, "It is necessary now and then for a man to go away by himself and experience loneliness; to sit on a rock in the forest and ask of himself, 'Who am I, and where have I been, and where am I going?'"

Finally, no visit to the site is complete without meeting the famous goat herd. The friendly farm staff awaits your arrival, and they are happy to answer questions about the three species of goats—Saanen, Toggenburg and Nubian—that live exceptionally charmed lives there. There are informational signs and displays in the barn about the goats and Lilian Sandburg's many accomplishments and accolades pertaining to them.

Grab a grooming brush near the fenced gate before you visit the goats in the pasture. Each animal wears a leather collar bearing its name, which starts with the first letter of its mother's name—a tradition started by Lilian. The goats are used to visitors and soak up the attention. A barn cat or two are usually perched somewhere close by, monitoring the scene. On a nice day, it's a hard place to leave.

CONTINUING EDUCATION

Bonesteel, Paul. *The Day Carl Sandburg Died*. Bonesteel Films, 2011.

Hendrick, George, and Willene Hendrick, eds. *Selected Poems by Carl Sandburg*. Ecco, 1996.

PART VII

URBAN TRAILS

These urban trails traverse paved paths instead of dirt ones, offering fantastic ways to explore a city and learn about its history and culture. Most are designed to pass near retail and dining establishments, which makes your outing even more fun.

The following are my favorite historic urban "hikes" in western North Carolina. For driving directions and logistical information, I've provided websites in the descriptions, as these routes have less-defined start and end points than a traditional backcountry trail.

Flatiron building and Asheville Urban Trail sculpture. *Photograph by the author.*

29
ASHEVILLE URBAN TRAILS

Art, history and the architecture of the Land of the Sky are highlighted on three self-guided walking routes in downtown Asheville. The Urban Trail, Architecture Trail and the South Slope Mural Trail are all delightful ways to spend an afternoon exploring the city. Though all three are special, the 1.7-mile Urban Trail is my top pick. A large portion of the Architecture Trail overlaps the Urban Trail's route if you'd like to explore both at once.

Spanning five periods, the Urban Trail is a 1.7-mile loop route that weaves through the city's downtown district. Thirty stations dot the trail, each recognizable by a sculpture, bronze plaque or local art highlighting Asheville's entertaining history and the achievements of recognizable residents, such as George Vanderbilt and F. Scott Fitzgerald, along with less-recognizable names, such as Elizabeth Blackwell, MD, the first woman to receive a medical degree in the United States.

For more information about the Asheville urban trails, including interactive and printable maps, visit www.exploreasheville.com/urban-trail/.

30

WAYNESVILLE PUBLIC ART TRAIL

Waynesville is the place I call home, so I am admittedly biased about this selection. But even if I wasn't a resident, I'd still recommend it. Per the Waynesville Public Art Trail website, this self-guided tour celebrates "the cultural heritage and natural wonders of the Southern Appalachians in the heart of Western North Carolina."

Seventeen art pieces dot the route through three districts: Hazelwood, Frog Level and downtown/Main Street. You can walk to all of the art pieces in one go, but I recommend driving to the Plott hound exhibit in Hazelwood, as it's the farthest away from the other sixteen pieces.

Old Time Music sculpture in downtown Waynesville. *Donna Lang.*

My personal favorite station is *Old Time Music*, which was cataloged by the Smithsonian for its symbolic folk art traits. This whimsical sculpture is situated a stone's throw from historic Main Street and its plethora of dining and retail businesses.

A fan favorite on Main Street, Mast General Store, began in Valle Crucis in 1883. Over time, the retailer has grown to support several locations, including this one. You'll feel as if you've stepped back in time as soon as your feet hit the creaky floorboards. Make sure to visit the lower level, whose candy barrels with many varieties of vintage candy are a hit with the young and old.

To learn more about the trail and find an interactive map, scavenger hunt and audio tour, visit the Waynesville Public Art Trail website at www.waynesvillepublicart.org/.

31
FRANKLIN WOMEN'S HISTORY TRAIL

Franklin, North Carolina, is a frequent town stop for Appalachian Trail thru hikers who need to refresh and resupply. Its popular outfitter, Outdoor 76, has a reputation for employing shoe experts who can help sojourners with blistered and battered feet find a new pair of kicks before they continue their trek.

Franklin has also put itself on the map with its engaging Women's History Trail (WHT), the first trail of its kind in North Carolina that is sponsored by the Folk Heritage Association of Macon County. According to the WHT website, "The trail weaves together the disparate elements of our heritage; those of all levels of society; those of pioneer stock and those more recently arrived, telling their stories through various art mediums/ exhibits and markers."

The most engaging exhibit is the newly unveiled sculpture *Sowing the Seeds of the Future*. Dedicated on March 24, 2024, the sculpture depicts a Cherokee woman, an enslaved woman and a pioneer woman, all touching hands to symbolize the sisterhood of women as they proudly keep watch over the Women's History Park.

These figures represent former women who were connected by property along the Little Tennesse River across from the Noquisiyi Mound, a cultural and spiritual center of the Cherokee. A nearby stone wall with embedded plaques conveys each woman's contribution and influence. The sculpture "is intended to acknowledge and celebrate women's contributions, to

Sowing the Seeds of the Future sculpture on the Women's History Trail. *Photograph by the author.*

inspire future generations of girls and women to pursue their dreams, and to challenge us all to learn from the past and aspire for a more equitable future."

To learn more and find the interactive map for the trail's various stations in Franklin, North Carolina, visit the Women's History Trail website at www.womenshistorytrail.org.

ABOUT THE AUTHOR

Nancy East retired after twenty-three years as a small animal veterinarian to focus on outdoor education and writing. An avid hiker and backpacker, she is also a certified Southern Appalachian Naturalist, a hiking guide and a dedicated member of the Haywood County Search and Rescue Team. The search for a missing mother in Great Smoky Mountains National Park inspired her record-setting hike and book, *Chasing the Smokies Moon: An Audacious 948-Mile Hike—Fueled by Love, Loss, Laughter, and Lunacy.* Nancy lives with her husband, three children and their beloved rescue dog in Lake Junaluska, North Carolina. Discover more about her work at nancyeast.com.